INSTITUTE OF CORNISH STUDIES

SOURCES OF CORNISH HISTORY

Volume one

EDITOR'S NOTE

The intention of this series is to introduce documentary material concerned with the history of Cornwall which has not been readily available to the general public. The objective is to present Cornish history within a wider setting and therefore this first volume includes regional material because the subject of harvest failure can only be understood by comparing Cornwall with Devon and the rest of England. This collection of documents raises many complex issues which it is hoped will be answered by those conducting intensive research on individual communities (whether parish, town or hamlet).

SOURCES OF CORNISH HISTORY

Volume 1

HARVEST FAILURE IN CORNWALL AND DEVON

the Book of Orders and the corn surveys of 1623 and 1630-1

Edited with an Introduction by

Todd Gray

1992

INSTITUTE OF CORNISH STUDIES

ISBN 0 903686 65 1

Printed for the Institute of Cornish Studies by
Latimer Trend & Company Ltd, Estover Close,
Plymouth, Devon, England

For Veronica and Frank,
with many thanks and much affection

CONTENTS

LIST OF TABLES

LIST OF MAPS

ILLUSTRATION

1. Cover illustration (by permission of British Library): 'Harvesting', Raphael
   Holinshed, *The Chronicles of England, Scotlande and Ireland* (1577)

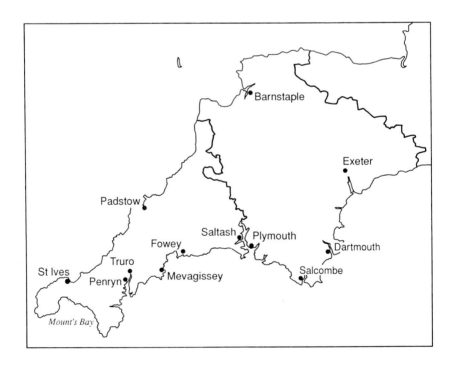

Cornwall and Devon

INTRODUCTION

Harvest failure, leading in some instances to famine, remains a world-wide problem especially when caused by droughts such as experienced recently in Africa. By contrast the last period of severe food shortages in Cornwall (and Devon) was probably during the 1590s, even then the consequences were not as serious as those caused by the great Irish famine of 1846-51.[1] The inhabitants of Elizabethan and early Stuart England, who did not exploit alternatives sources of protein such as rice or the potato, depended mainly upon supplies of grain for the central part of their general diet in the form of either bread or beer. Although food riots continued to occur occasionally, as in the rest of England, the early seventeenth century was a turning point in the country's ability to feed itself. The harvest failure of 1622 has been regarded as the last year in which there was large-scale starvation in England.[2] However, there was also a major harvest failure in 1608, and again in 1630, in the South West as well as throughout the country.

Somewhat surprisingly, dearth[3] (high prices resulting from relative scarcity) was not always regarded as being detrimental. Richard Carew wrote in his *Survey of Cornwall* of 1602 that

I have been always prone to maintain a paradox, that dearth of corn in Cornwall... so it go not accompanied with a scarcity, is no way prejudicial to the country and I am induced thus to think, for the reasons ensuing: there are no two trades which set so many hands on work, at all times of the year, as that one of tillage: the husbandman finding profit herein is encouraged to bestow pains and charges for enclosing and dressing of waste grounds, which there through afterwards become also good for pasture. With the ready money gotten by his weekly selling of corn, he setteth the artificer on work, who were better to buy dear bread,being but a part of his meat, and which he countervaileth again, by raising the price of his ware, than to sit idly, knocking his heels against the wall.[4]

Carew's belief was that high corn prices, which were caused by minor corn shortages, encouraged farmers to cultivate waste land and thereby employment was not only increased, but subsequently the general economy was stimulated.

In 1630 what had seemed paradoxical to Carew was once again an issue of considerable discussion in Cornwall. As will be seen below, the effects of an

xi

indifferent harvest that year were enhanced by the region's traditional interest in, and in some places dependence upon, the coastal and overseas fisheries. The shortfall of the harvest was the result of natural causes, but the actual scarcities of corn were man-made: there was a conflict of interest between the general population which was dependent upon local grain supplies and the corn merchants who were selling their wheat and barley to victuallers throughout Cornwall, the South West and other parts of the country.

In the most original and stimulating work on English famine to date, Dr Andrew Appleby concluded that the 'necessary environment' for research on harvest failure is a regional study because 'famine can only be understood properly when it is solidly placed in its social and economic context'.[5] This volume concentrates on the harvest failures in Cornwall and Devon and seeks to show that the causes of the Cornish shortages, and the ability to withstand them, particularly in 1630, were very localized in their nature. The government's general policy was to prevent corn shortages from resulting in an escalation of prices beyond the means of the general population, but the state was even more anxious that undersupply did not develop into famine. The correspondence which resulted from the government's measures form the principal body of the documents printed here, and it is through this material that the local aspect of the harvest failures can be understood. Because the character of the Cornish conditions cannot be fully measured except in its regional context, correspondence from Devon is also printed.[6] Moreover, its inclusion is particularly appropriate because of the fortunate survival of a survey of two hundreds in south Devon which is comparable to one of Pydar hundred in north Cornwall. There are few other surveys for the rest of England of this date containing such detailed information on the size of rural households.

THE COMPILATION OF THE CERTIFICATES AND THEIR INTERPRETATION

The early Stuart government's response to the corn shortages, and to the prospect of civil unrest, was to issue administrative instructions to the county justices which were intended to assess the extent of local shortages and ensure that there were sufficient corn supplies in the markets. The government's *Book of Orders* on dearth was similar to others which were concerned with such issues as plague, sports and poverty. The *Book of Orders* on dearth was first published in 1586 but incorporated earlier similar measures of the early sixteenth century. It was reissued in 1594, 1595, 1608, 1622 and 1630.[7] That of 1608 (83) was reprinted in 1622 but in 1630 it was reissued with alterations.

The Privy Council instructed each High Sheriff to present the county justices with a copy of the *Book of Orders*. Included in the orders were directions to restrict the use of corn, regulate the price and availability of all grain in the markets, suppress unnecessary alehouses and oversee the movement of corn supplies. In order to assess the local conditions, the justices were obliged to meet first in small groups within their local area, whether a 'hundred, rape or wapentake'.[8] The Cornish justices were divided into four divisions: east (East and West hundreds), west (Kerrier and Penwith), south (Powder and Pydar) and north (Trigg, Lesnewth and Stratton).[9] Only one example can be found where they appear to have deviated from the traditional division: the certificates were all based on the ancient hundred boundaries with the exception of East hundred which was divided into two divisions, the north and the south.(**67,71**) Although in several letters there was an emphasis on the ancient custom of the Devon divisions there was some confusion (such as with the hundred of Stanborough) over where the boundaries lay.(**9,11**) The inclusion of parishes within any one particular division appears to have been a discretionary decision rather than a historical one. In addition, at times some justices did not meet in a division but in a miscellaneous collection of hundreds.[10]

The material printed in this volume consists of the certificates sent from Cornwall and Devon in response to the governmental enquiries into the local conditions in the national harvest failures of 1622 and 1630. Some reports of 1631 have been included because enquiries into the harvest of 1630 continued for several more years.

The justices' reports form the greater part of the documentation printed. For Cornwall, there survives for 1623 certificates for Kerrier, Lesnewth, Penwith and Trigg hundreds and for 1630-31 for the hundreds of Lesnewth, Pydar, Stratton, Trigg and part of East. There are no extant certificates from Powder or West hundreds for either 1623 or 1630-31 although there is some correspondence from two justices in West hundred in 1630. For Devon, reports survive for 1623 for the hundreds of Black Torrington, Coleridge, Crediton, Exminster, Hartland, Haytor, Lifton, North Tawton, Roborough, South Molton, Stanborough, Tavistock, Teignbridge, West Budleigh, Witheridge and Wonford hundreds. For 1630-31 they exist for Axminster, Bampton, Cliston, Coleridge, Colyton, East Budleigh, Ermington, Exminster, Halberton, Hayridge, Haytor, Hemyock, Lifton, North Tawton, Ottery St Mary, Plympton, Roborough, Stanborough, Tavistock, Teinbridge, Tiverton, Witheridge and Wonford hundreds. There are no surviving certificates from the justices in the hundreds of Braunton, Fremington, Shebbear or Shirwell for either 1623 or 1630-31.

The sheriffs appear to have sent the justices' certificates to the Privy Council as they were received and the lack of surviving returns may mean that they were unable to produce them. This, as well as the brevity and repetitive form of some of the certificates, could be interpreted as an indication that there was some local resistance on the part of the justices to the imposition of this *Book of Orders*.[11] However, it is apparent that some certificates have not survived (**64**) and the recurring format of some letters may have been due only to the particular style of the scribe.(**58 & 60, 45-7**)

THE PARISH SURVEYS OF THE CORNISH HUNDRED OF PYDAR AND DEVON HUNDREDS OF COLERIDGE AND STANBOROUGH

The justices, after consulting within their division, had to arrange for the assessment of local conditions. In order to accurately appraise this they were instructed to call before them the high and petty constables as well as up to 36 of 'the most honest and substantial inhabitants' of each parish.(**83**) The number of these parishioners, the 'jury' as they were termed in several certificates,(**45-7**) varied throughout Cornwall and Devon: for example, in one division it was claimed to have involved two or three of the 'substantial inhabitants of every parish' (**7**) and while the justices claimed that in another division they had the constables and one parishioner view the parish (**11**), the actual reports show there was a considerable variation in the number of individuals who signed their names to their surveys.(**12-41**)

The justices' certificates form the majority of the south-western reports (as they do nationally) but there are also a few surviving original parish surveys: there is a brief report of the parish of Tiverton in May 1631,(**72**) certificates from five boroughs regarding corn supplies and the suppression of alehouses in February 1623,(**1-5**) and most significantly, there are separate reports for the parishes of Pydar hundred in north Cornwall in 1630 and Coleridge and Stanborough hundreds in south Devon in 1623.(**57,12-41**) The surveys of the three hundreds are unusual among the certificates which were returned for the rest of the country in that they listed the total number of persons in each household surveyed.

The report of the Cornish hundred of Pydar, signed in early December 1630 by John Prideaux of Prideaux Place in Padstow and Edward Coswarth of Coswarth in the parish of Colan, comprises twenty parish surveys. The only report missing is that of Colan. The first part of the survey recorded details of the grain-producers, or holders, while the second listed malsters, brewers, tipplers, bakers, engrossers and forestallers.

The surveys of the Devon hundreds of Coleridge and Stanborough were probably made during the first part of February 1623 (only that for the parish of Dartington of 8 February is dated) and comprise a series of individual parish reports, many of which were signed by the petty constables and 'raters'. Altogether there are 31 surveys. These reports do not cover all the parishes in the two hundreds: it appears as though Dean Prior, Buckfastleigh and Holne were in a different administrative division of the justices.(**9**) Also, there is no survey for the parish of Slapton and two boroughs (Dartmouth and Totnes) are not included, although a separate certificate was sent from Dartmouth during the same month.(**2**)

The constables were instructed to exclude from the 'jury' selection 'such [householders] as be known great farmers for corn, or that store of grain to sell'. The parishioners were to appraise the corn held by 'every householder that hath corn in their barns, stacks or other where, as well Justices of the Peace as others whatsoever'.(83) Many of those surveyed were the 'yeomen' of the parish but there were also gentlemen, husbandmen and others. One of the householders was James Cundy of Padstow who described himself in his will as a blacksmith; his probate inventory recorded not only his 'smithing tools' but one cow, nine sheep and wheat in the ground.[12] Most of the householders were male but there were also forty-five women, of whom the majority were noted as being widows.

Some individuals were listed as not having kept a household. But at least a few of these were men, some of whom were merchants, who resided outside the parish. For example, Arthur Stribley of Little Petherick kept grain in the neighbouring parish of St Issey.(57) Likewise, John Chubb of Salcombe, probably a sailor and ship-owner of that haven,[13] kept 60 bushels of wheat and barley across the Kingsbridge estuary in the parish of South Pool(36) and Arthur Harrell of Woodleigh had in the parish of North Huish one 'mowhay' containing 100 bushels of wheat and barley and another mowhay which held 80 bushels of oats.(24) More intriguing are the details of Richard Rich, a merchant who maintained his household in Blackawton where he farmed. In addition, he had 30 bushels of wheat, barley and oats in Kingsbridge, kept in one 'Lady Harrice's barton' within Cornworthy parish, a further 200 bushels of corn, and he tilled there 3 acres of barley and 16 of wheat.(32,22,40) These holdings are indicative of the broad pattern of farming whereby individuals worked land outside their resident parishes.

There is a sizable difference in the number of householders recorded between each parish survey: while the report for St Breock listed 48 individuals that for Little Petherick had only one.(57) The difference must generally reflect the diverse number of grain-producers in each parish. But it should not be assumed that all the principal grain producers in any of the three hundreds were included in the parish surveys. It is interesting that Edward Coswarth, one of the signatories to the Pydar survey in 1630, was accused only two years earlier of unfairly exempting Lord Lambert and John Arundel of Trerise, two of the most influential men in Pydar hundred, from inclusion in a subsidy.[14] Also, it is intriguing that, as noted earlier, the report of Colan parish, where Coswarth resided, is missing. Other individuals may well have been left out as well, as they were in other parts of the country,[15] possibly due to corruption or simply because at that particular time they did not have corn remaining in their granaries.

The reports are not reliable indicators of average grain planting for several reasons. It is not always clear whether the report recorded the total amount of grain held or merely the owner's spare supply. Production must have been disrupted by the previous year's shortages and while in some parishes this may have prompted increased tillage there were some complaints that there were difficulties with obtaining seed corn. Virtually all of the Cornish or Devon surveys merely recorded the planting of barley and oats. The amount of wheat acreage was noted only in the Loddiswell parish survey. This was because the survey was concerned with the amount of available grain, including seed corn, and as wheat had been sown in the previous autumn, unlike barley or oats which were generally sown later, a note of wheat acreage was superfluous to their recording purposes. Curiously, the surveys rarely included beans which were noted in many reports in other counties. Only occasionally were bushels of peas listed, the most notable example of this being the survey for Ashprington,(**39**) and there is only one mention of the number of acres planted with peas: one Steven Wemoth of Cornworthy had 6 acres sown with peas.(**40**)

The surveys must be seen as generally recording only a portion of the total arable acreage. The figures do however provide a general indication of the size of land holdings. For Loddiswell parish the number of acres planted with wheat, barley and oats ranged from one and a half acres to 63 but there was no consistent ratio of acres of wheat to those of barley or oats.(**23**) For the parish of Halwell the amount of acres to be sown (presumably just of oats and barley) ranged from 10 to 35 acres with the mean average being 19.9 acres.(**41**) The difference in the size of acreages between individuals no doubt reflected the wide range of those included in the surveys. Thus, the number of arable acres should be perceived as being a portion of the overall farm size: few would not also have had pastoral land which many probably concentrated on. It should also be remembered that there was a difference between the size of Cornish and English acres, the Cornish acre being slightly larger than that of the English. Household holdings of bushels of grain are also not indicative of an average year's holding not only because the harvest yield was poor but also because holdings were probably depleted by greater sales.

FARMING IN CORNWALL AND DEVON

In the early seventeenth century Cornwall and Devon were principally pastoral counties, particularly in the Cornish parishes around Bodmin and the western moorland and in Devon on the higher grounds near Dartmoor and Exmoor. Both counties produced extensive quantities of wool, particularly Devon, but the Cornish economy was much less dependent upon the cloth industry. There was in both, however, a mixed agrarian economy. Although many farms concentrated on the raising of sheep, and cattle, few were not also involved with other livestock, such as pigs and poultry, and tilled grain and, in many areas, grew fruit. Few, if any, could afford to specialize in only one single form of husbandry. There was an increasing cultivation of what previously had been waste land, but by this period much of the region was already enclosed (if indeed it had ever been open) but not all. For example, when the churchwardens surveyed the parish of St Merryn in Pydar hundred in 1646 it was noted that 'this survey was made before it was hedged'.[16] In some places crops were still grown in open strips. Braunton Great Field may be the best known but open fields existed in other parishes as well. In 1626 Edward Welsh of Halwill parish in north-west Devon had, in a close called the Middle Park, 'certain ground divided by *landshare* [sic] where he himself had oats grown'.[17]

There was a great diversity of agrarian activity in what is a very large region. Proximity to population centres no doubt stimulated market-gardening: the 80 cabbages said to be growing in Heavitree in 1622 were doubtless intended for the nearby market of Exeter.[18] Of course, the remoteness of other parishes must have slowed such development. The richness of the soil of some areas, such as that in the Vale of Exeter, contrasts with the poorer farm land over many other parts of the South West: in the Penwith peninsula, where the land is high and relatively barren, it would have been more common for a small-holder to have kept a goat for household milk than a cow.

The principal arable crops were wheat, barley, oats and to a much lesser extent, rye. It is known that there were at least two types of wheat grown in Cornwall: a 'bearded' variety was planted on the best land and 'knotweed', which had a lower yield, was grown on poor soil.[19] In both Cornwall and Devon 'small' oats, or pillas, had long been grown[20] but it is not clear how extensively it was cultivated in the early seventeenth century. Rye was a crop of secondary importance. Certainly it was not mentioned in the Pydar survey and does not seem to have been exported from Padstow. It was sown in small acreages and only on the poorest ground such as in the parish of Altarnun on Bodmin Moor.(72) One of the few probate inventories for Pydar hundred which mentions rye is that of John Benny of St Mawgan in 1615. Even so, his inventory also included wheat, barley and oats.[21] Eight parishes in the South Hams surveys included references to rye,(24,30-3,35,38,41) but the justices of these hundreds wrote of it that in their markets 'none or little is sold'.(79) It had a secondary use as thatch.[22] Of course, the crops which were planted altered from one parish to another, depending upon the quality of the land. Beans and peas were also widely grown in many parts of the region, but in some areas, such as in the hundreds of Witheridge, South Molton and North Tawton in north to mid-Devon, they were said to not 'agree' with the soil there.(42) There are no references in the certificates to the growing of either lentils or rape seed in either Cornwall or Devon, though these crops were planted in some other parts of England.[23]

John Leland's impression of Cornwall in the first part of the sixteenth century was of an uneven landscape of rich cultivated land and barren wasteland and Devon was held by him in only slightly better regard. In sharp contrast, little more than a hundred years later Oliver Cromwell is said to have remarked (upon what must have been only a passing familiarity) on the advanced state of Devon's agriculture.[24] Carew thought that the Cornish had neglected husbandry in favour of their tin workings but because the mines had begun to fail, and also because of an increase in population, they had been constrained to return to agriculture and had since become very proficient at it. Certainly as late as 1572 it was claimed, albeit regarding purveyance, that Cornwall could not produce enough corn for its needs but regularly imported grain from other counties.[25] In regards to his native Devon Hooker thought that it was not remarkable for growing grain but was 'like others for corn of all sorts wheat, rye, barley, oats, pulses, vetches'.[26]However, both Carew and Hooker noted the great agrarian improvements made in their counties which had changed them from importers to exporters of foodstuffs. They recognised the key to the region's success: Cornwall and Devon had become by that time widely known for the techniques used in improving the land. These included the process locally known as 'beating', but in other places as 'Devonshiring', in which turf was cut, burnt and the ashes spread upon the land. Other materials were also used to improve the soil (dependent upon the area) including dung, marl, soap ashes, lime and 'in some places they have a kind of slime or sea sand... there is no dung to be compared unto it'. Many places in Cornwall had a 'sand way' where the sand was carried several miles from the shore to the fields. One such lane was at Burgois in St Issey where sand was brought up the river Camel from the mouth of the river and presumably landed at Salt Water Mill. Ore-weed was used for improving land for barley.[27] Land improvement was promoted by national writers in the early seventeenth century but by that time was already a long-standing practice in Cornwall and Devon.[28]

Against this general background the three principal surveys, of Pydar hundred in 1630 and of the two hundreds in the South Hams in 1623 (see maps 2 & 3), contain some detailed information about arable farming in what were two greatly different areas.

PYDAR HUNDRED

It is clear from the parish returns of Pydar hundred that there was a considerable amount of barley and wheat grown there. The land in the middle of the county was poorer for the growing of corn not only because it was higher and hillier but also because of the weather the harvest was later than the rest of the county.[29] John Norden, whose *Topographical and Historical Description of Cornwall* was greatly, though not wholly, derived from Carew's *Survey of Cornwall*, wrote that the chief agricultural areas were the hundreds bordering Devon as well as those on the south coast, with the exception of Penwith in the far west. Carew did not particularly note Pydar for corn-growing but did write that the area immediately bordering Pydar, between Bodmin and the north coast, was a 'fruitful vein of land, comprising several parishes, which serveth better than any other place in Cornwall for winter feeding'.[30]

The Cornish had increased their tillage of barley in place of oats and barley was, with wheat, the preferred crop. While the parish reports of Pydar confirm this, other evidence shows that oats, peas, beans and rye were also grown: for example, Thomas Pellian of Newlyn East grew wheat, barley, peas and oats and John Spark of St Columb Minor grew peas and beans. As mentioned earlier there is no apparent ratio between the types of corn grown and one reason must be crop rotation. Gilbert Cayser of St Mawgan-in-Pydar was recorded in 1632 as having 13 acres of wheat and 3 acres of oats; Richard Collinge of Roscarreck, Lanivet, was noted as having sowed by July 1616 14 acres of wheat, 4 acres of barley and 13 acres of oats; Thomas Hicks, also of Lanivet, had in 1640 8 acres of oats, 7 acres of barley and 7 acres of wheat. The inventories show mixed farming in Pydar as well. That of John Watts of St Columb Minor, proved in 1632, recorded not only that the corn in his mowhay and ground was worth more than £250, but that his livestock included 24 draught oxen, 21 cows, 2 bulls, 7 'labouring' horses and 540 sheep. Watts was a farmer of some considerable worth and status: the survey of Pydar noted that his household stood at 24 persons and in his will he provided £1200 to be divided between his eight daughters and left instructions that they were to be 'brought up in learning as is fit and necessary for children of their discretion and degree'. Likewise, Thomas Vivian of Crantock, with a smaller household of ten persons, owned at the time of his death livestock including oxen, bullocks, cows, sheep, horses and pigs and also 22 acres of wheat. The livestock of many others, such as Thomas Dungy, likewise of Crantock, also included geese, guinea fowl and hens. Hops were also grown: Richard Courtney of Lanivet had two hop-gardens at the time of his death in 1633. Bee-keeping was also wide-spread and every parish must have had some bee-keepers. The probate inventory of Ambrose Lawry of St Columb Major in 1613 listed 10 bee hives and 13 buts of bees. St Issey could boast of having its own beehive-maker; at least one George Braysie of that parish claimed to have that occupation, if it could have been a full-time one, in 1637.[31]

COLERIDGE AND STANBOROUGH HUNDREDS

Tristram Risdon believed that there were great similarities between Devon and Cornwall. He wrote of Devon that

> it swells up with many hills, which cause as low valleys, in that respect much resembling Cornwall, with which it was formerly united in one province, and which I admit into fellowship, not only for its vicinity and affinity but also for the similar dispositions of the inhabitants both in body and mind, in which ancient authors make little distinction between them.[32]

Certainly in many ways farming in the South Hams was very similar to that in Pydar hundred. According to Alexander Grosse, preacher at Plympton St Mary, the county of Devon

> may not be unfitly resembled to a large piece of coarse kersey, enbordered with a rich fringe of gold. All the outskirts of this county, especially to the south and west, are a very rich soil, but what lieth within these borders is a most coarse and barren earth, called by the natives the moors, generally waste and forest lands.[33]

The South Hams were Grosse's 'golden fringe' of the county and the area Risdon termed the 'garden of Devonshire'. Not only is the ground richer but the climate is more sheltered, warmer and dryer than in Pydar and in most of Cornwall and Devon. At the time of the survey the fields were being ploughed in preparation for sowing.(38) The parish surveys confirm the unpopularity of rye which had not been a prevailing crop in this part of Devon for some considerable time.[34] The surveys listed considerable holdings of wheat and the few surviving probate inventories for south Devon show, as those do for Pydar, a preference for the cultivation of wheat and barley.[35] Finally, in the South Hams it is likely that fruit-growing was more widespread, particularly of apples for cider-making.

Dartmoor provided valuable summer grazing of livestock, both cattle and sheep. Mixed farming was as traditional in the South Hams as in other parts of Devon. Farmers in south Devon were closer to a greater number of markets which were also more vibrant than those in north Cornwall. Not only were they between Exeter and Plymouth, but they were near such towns as Ashburton, Totnes, Kingsbridge and Salcombe. Proximity to the latter, and to Dartmouth, must have stimulated the growing of arable crops. It will be discussed below how Plymouth and Dartmouth were centres for the overseas fisheries and considerable amounts of grain were needed for victualling the fishing fleet. There were also the demands of the native merchant fleet as well as of foreign ships. Finally, Plymouth was being used increasingly to victual the ships of the Royal Navy, particularly in the wars of the 1620s. It was because of these demands that south Devon was an importer of grain. Considerable amounts of grain were brought into Dartmouth for victualling the shipping there: for example, from 1612 to 1615 wheat, barley, rye, oatmeal and beans were imported from ports in France, the Low Countries and Ireland.[36] These imports do not signify a deficiency in grain production in the South Hams but rather the vitality of the overseas fisheries.

SIZE OF HOUSEHOLDS

The parish reports of the three hundreds of Pydar, Coleridge and Stanborough recorded the total number of members in each household that produced corn. The instructions given in the *Book of Orders* were to record those who were 'great' farmers for corn, or that had a store of grain, 'what number of persons of every householder ... have in their houses feeding, lying and uprising or otherwise to be fed'.(83) These were the grain-producers of the parish and the surveys did not list those who were only consumers. There was a difference in the way in which these households were recorded between the Cornish and Devon reports. The survey of Pydar hundred simply listed a figure under a column headed 'persons', and the report itself is entitled 'the number of persons which are in the houses of every householder'. But the parish reports from the South Hams are more informative, particularly in regard to the degree to which the parish constables and raters or 'viewers of the corn' understood their instructions. For many of the parish reports the number of occupants were listed merely as 'persons' but there were many descriptive differences. The survey of Dodbrooke noted each individual's 'persons in his house', and those of South Milton, Churchstow and Woodleigh recorded the 'people to house'. The report of East Portlemouth was headed 'A note how many persons every man hath in his house', and that for Loddiswell 'A note what people every person here underwritten hath in his house'. The survey of Charleton was headed 'their household', and the individuals were listed for 'this many in their houses'. Likewise, the report for Rattery was headed 'how many people are in their houses', and that for South Pool was headed 'the number of persons in each men's house'. The reports of Blackawton and Stoke Fleming were of each man's 'company'. But most significantly, the survey for South Brent was headed 'the number of company every of them keep in their houses besides workmen'.(15,21,16-18,26,34,36,32,38,30) In some instances the number given for each household must have included day-labourers and was not limited to the 'family' which at this time included kin as well as servants. Servants were generally unmarried, hired for at least a year and lodged under the master's roof while day-labourers received wages and were resident elsewhere.[37]

There was a considerable difference in the number of persons in each household. The two largest households were both of 40 persons: these were those of Thomas Mundy of St Columb Minor and of Arthur Champernowne of Dartington Hall.(57,33) The smallest household listed was that of Christopher Cardoll of Perranzabuloe which had only one member.(57) In total there were 260 households recorded for Pydar hundred, with the total number of members being 2,802 persons, and 379 households in the two hundreds of Devon which had 3,848 residents. The average mean number of each household was 9.3 persons for Pydar hundred, 9.8 persons for Coleridge and Stanborough hundreds and 9.6 persons overall.

Peter Laslett estimated that in pre-industrial England there was a mean household size of 4.75 but that this varied between social groups. He concluded that 'a majority of all persons lived in the larger households in traditional England, those above 6 persons in size, in spite of the fact that only a third of all households were in this category and that the overall mean household size was less than five'.[38] There was also a distinct difference in household size between types of communities: it has been estimated that there was a mean household size in Cambridge in the 1620s of 4.13 persons. It has also been estimated that there was a correlation between wealth and size of households: those of gentlemen standing at 8.63 persons while that of labourers at 3.65.[39] The poorest households were clearly small, some urban censuses showing that they generally averaged between two to three persons although there could be strong local variations.[40] The variation of household size in the early seventeenth century reports of the three hundreds of Cornwall and Devon likewise reflects the diversity of the householders' economic and social status. There were many gentlemen listed who, as would be expected, had the largest households. Altogether there were 57 householders who were given the title of either gentleman, esquire or 'Mr'. These individuals had a mean household size of 18.4 persons. In comparison, the two men described as 'clerks' who were noted as having households, John Coad of St Ervan, and Peter Blake of St Breock, had

Table 1 HOUSEHOLDS IN PYDAR HUNDRED, 1630

	number of persons in households																																	number of house-holds	number in house-holds	parish pop.[1] 1642	per cent of pop.
	1	2	3	4	5	6	7	8	9	10	11	12	13	14	15	16	17	18	19	20	21	22	23	24	25	26	27	28	30	32	34	36	40				
St Breock	1	2	1	4	4	2	1	4	6	1	3	3	2	2	2				1															42	420	623	67.4
Padstow	2	4	2	3		6	3		2	2	1	4		1																				31	295	693	42.6
St Issey		1	1		1	2	2	1	2	1	3	1	3	2																				20	206	445	46.3
St Merryn	1	1		1	1	1		1	2	2	1		1											1										14	164	335	49.0
St Columb Minor	1	1		2	3	2	6	7	1	3	1	3		2										1	1							1		35	412	740	55.7
Newlyn East						1	1	2	3	1	1																							11	94	570	16.5
Cubert		1	2	1	1	1	1	3	1	1	2							2																14	159	280	56.8
Crantock	1	2		2		2	4	4	3		4			1				1																18	152	333	45.6
St Enoder					1			1																										4	60	438	13.7
Lanivet		1	1	1		1	1	2	1	2	1	2	1	1	1										1									13	153	465	32.9
Perranzabuloe	1	1	1	1	1	1		2	1	2																		2						11	95	493	20.9
Mawgan-in-Pydar	1	1					1	1	3													1												9	141	353	39.9
St Agnes								1		1																								1	12	353	4.2
St Wenn	1				1	1		2	1	2	1	1		2									1		1									12	168	288	58.3
Withiel									1	1																								2	26	233	11.2
Lanhydrock		1			1		1	2	1		1										1													4	44	168	26.2
St Eval		1	1				2	1	1																									6	51	200	25.5
St Ervan		1	2			3			1		1							1																3	28	220	12.7
St Columb Major					1				3					1															1					9	102	918	11.1
Little Petherick																	1																	1	20	70	28.6
Total	1	3	7	17	10	18	17	28	23	33	9	28	5	14	7	11	2	8	6	2		2	1	1	1	5		1	1			1	1	260	2802	8320	33.6

1. Source for general population estimates (based on a multiplier of 2.5 persons per signature of the Protestation Returns): T.L. Stoate (ed.), *Cornwall Protestation Returns* (Bristol, 1974); A.J. Howard (ed.), *Devon Protestation Returns* (Bristol, 1973).

Table 2   HOUSEHOLDS IN COLERIDGE AND STANBOROUGH HUNDREDS, 1623

number of persons in households

	1	2	3	4	5	6	7	8	9	10	11	12	13	14	15	16	17	18	19	20	21	22	23	24	25	26	27	28	30	32	34	36	40				
W. Alvington	1	1	2	1	1	4	2	2	1	1	1	2		2							1													23	254	435	56.1
E. Allington	2		2	1	2	3	2	2	1		1	1																			1			17	147	300	49.0
Harberton		1	3	1	1	1	3	1	1		1	1		1						1												1		15	144	765	18.8
Dodbrooke	1		2		1	2						1																						6	44	325	13.5
Churchstow		1		1	1	1	1	1		1					1																			8	92	168	54.7
Woodleigh	1		1		1	1	1	1	1	1		1											1	1										8	101	180	56.1
E. Portlemouth	1		3	4	1		1	1		1				1					1															11	84	175	48.0
Sherford		1	1	1		1	1	1	1																			1						8	98	300	32.6
Moreleigh		1	1		1	1				1	1		1						1															6	74	118	62.7
S. Milton	2	1	3	1		1	1	2		1	2					1																		11	97	198	48.9
Kingsbridge	1	1																																2	13	378	3.4
Loddiswell			1	2		1		3		1	1		2	1		1 1 1				1														11	163	363	44.9
N. Huish			1	2		1			1		1		1	1	1																	1		10	128	250	51.2
S. Huish	1					3				3	1		1																					6	70	285	24.6
Charleton	1	3	4		3	7	3	3	2	1		1		1			1																	29	216	378	57.1
Stokenham	1	1	2	1		6	3	2	2	1	1	2		1																				23	210	983	21.4
Thurlestone	1	4			3	3	5	1		2	1													1										25	224	255	87.8
Malborough	1		1	2	2	3	4	2	1	2	2	2	1				1																	23	244	760	31.9
S. Brent		2	2	4	1	2				3 1 1																								19	219	668	32.8
Diptford			3		3	2	1	1		1	1																							9	88	393	22.4
Blackawton		1	1	1	1		2	1		3	1																	1						12	141	708	19.9
Dartington						1	3										1														1			7	107	463	23.1
Rattery	1				2	1	1			1																								7	57	385	14.8
Dittisham	3	1				1	1	1		1				1			1					1												11	112	360	31.1
S. Pool		3			5	1	2	2	2	1																								18	190	240	79.2
Chivelstone	1	1				1	2	3		3																								11	111	290	38.3
Stoke Fleming		1			2		1	2	2			1								1			1											11	128	383	33.4
Ashprington					2	1	4			1	1	1																						11	104	353	29.5
Cornworthy	1					2	1	2																										6	43	388	11.1
Halwell	1	2				1	2	1	2		1	4			1 1 1					1														15	145	255	56.9
Total	3	7	18	22	33	34	58	31	37	18	41	8	11	10	15	3	5	1	9	1	3	1	1	1	1			2			1 1	2	1	379	3848	11502	33.4
Overall Totals	1	6	14	35	32	51	51	86	54	70	27	69	13	25	17	26	5	13	1	15	3	3	1	3	1	1	1	2	1	2	1 2	2	2	639	6650	19822	33.5

4 and 8 persons respectively.(57) Only one vicar was listed as such, that of the parish of Rattery, and his household surprisingly comprised ten persons.(34) There were 45 women recorded as being the heads of their households, including 28 who were noted as being widowed. Their household size ranged from 2 to 24 persons and the mean household size was 8.3 persons.

It is uncertain what proportion of the total population the surveys of the three hundreds recorded: what was the ratio of 'grain-producers' to 'grain-consumers'? Certainly the poorest households were not included. The table's last column shows a comparison between the total number of members of each parish's households and the parish population estimated from the Protestation Returns of 1642. The result is inconclusive because there is no obvious overall ratio. There could have been several reasons for this. First, the makeup of the population of each parish may have differed greatly from one to another: involvement in other industries, mining in St Agnes or fishing in Padstow, for example, may have altered the structure and composition of the work-force. Secondly, the formula used in estimating population may not be sophisticated enough to project an accurate population figure. Finally, it is possible that either the surveys or the Protestation Returns, or both, were not accurate.

It is not clear how accurately the household sizes were recorded. The number given both by Mundy and Champernowne could have been an approximate figure, as could have many of the others. It appears as though some individuals may have been listed twice: Elizabeth Hurrell, widow, appears in the reports for both Woodleigh and Moreleigh parishes. Moreover, in the first parish her household was recorded as being of 22 persons but in the second it stood at 12 persons. John Hurrell had a household recorded as 9 persons in one parish and 10 persons in another.(17,20) The details of the size of corn stocks and acreage are also considerably different when they can be compared. The duplicate listing was probably caused by the confusing boundaries of the parishes: not only were they neighbouring parishes but each had outlying territory situated beyond the other parish.

Notwithstanding, probate inventories of some of the Cornish householders provide supporting evidence for the very large size of some households. That for William Emmett, a Padstow yeoman, made in 1646, shows he had one bedstead with two featherbeds in the parlour, a bedstead with its flockbed in the chamber over the parlour, a trucklebed in the chamber over the hall, one bedstead with two featherbeds in the chamber over the buttery, two bedsteads and two featherbeds in 'the broad chamber over the way', one bedstead in the chamber over the kitchen and, finally, two bedsteads in 'Rosicleere Nation's chambers'; a provision for at least fourteen persons. He was recorded in the Pydar survey as having had a household of 12. Other inventories show that the number of beds correspond exactly to the reported household: William Roberts of St Columb Minor owned in 1626 six featherbeds and one trucklebed and his widow's household stood, four years later, at seven persons. One inventory shows more beds than the household number.[41] Although we can only guess at the ratio of persons to beds the high number of beds in these houses does indicate a substantial number of residents. It is not uncommon to find in probate inventories a room called 'the men's chamber'.[42] It is probable that there was in most farms at least one room permanently used for the housing of indentured servants.

There are only a few indications of extended households. In the report for St Breock parish 'Christopher Pedlar and his mother' had a household of 13 persons.(57) The survey of Dartington noted that 'Thomas Even and William Even [have]... 8 persons to house'.(33) In the report of Malborough it was noted that 'John and Richard Adams have in their house 18 persons' and also 'John Adam and Robert his son have in their house 12 persons'.(29)[43] The Loddiswell survey, which has a total of 12 households, has three similar entries: 'Simon Phillipps and his two sons have 26 [persons]' in their household, 'John Lovecraft and his two sons have 19' and 'John Gill and his son have 16'.(23) It is possible that these families lived in small hamlets and that for their own convenience the surveyors combined the recording of the households but it may also have been that there were households with three generations or more.

The total number of occupants in the households in the three hundreds of Cornwall and Devon demonstrates that there was a extensive range of individuals involved as grain-producers. It also shows that in these rural areas the household size of those with farming interests was far greater than that of other households, notably urban areas.[44] In addition, the considerable differences in household size shown here raise disturbing questions about the value and reliability of recording solely the mean size of households for particular communities.

HARVEST FAILURES IN EARLY STUART CORNWALL AND DEVON

There were poor harvests throughout England from 1594 to 1597, in 1608, in 1622, intermittently throughout the 1630s and during the late 1640s. The severity differed regionally and this was greatly determined by local climatic variations. Dearth was anticipated by unfavourable weather and rising prices, whether a harvest failure occurred or not. The South West peninsula is warmer in the winter than other parts of Great Britain but, as Carew noted, spring arrives later in Cornwall and the summers are not as warm. Within Cornwall there are also slight differences in climate: the far west and the northern coast, being more exposed, are traditionally far windier than the relatively more sheltered south coast. In regard to the weather of the two principal areas surveyed, Pydar hundred has a wetter climate than that of the South Hams. Notwithstanding these differences it is possible, to a certain extent, to reconstruct the general weather patterns of the South West in the early seventeenth century from notes made by three resident diarists. These are Philip Wyot of Barnstaple (who wrote between 1586 and 1608), William Whiteway of Dorchester (1618-35) and Sir Walter Yonge of Colyton (1604-28).[45] The application of the notes to events helps us to understand the weather patterns and clarify the local extent of the crop failures.

There were good harvests in 1590 and particularly in 1599 but unusually wet weather from 1595 to 1597 contributed to three consecutive poor harvests. The severity is indicated by measures taken by Devon's county justices: in April 1594 they granted licences to several men to transport corn, butter and cheese out of Somerset into Devon; the following year several badgers (middlemen between the producer and consumer) were allowed to bring wheat into Plymouth, and later Plympton, from the nearby markets of Dodbrooke, Kingsbridge and Modbury; the justices also licensed badgers to transport peas and beans from the Exeter and Newton Bushel markets to Totnes and Richard Hawkes of Rewe was permitted to bring corn, butter and cheese from Somerset and Dorset into any part of Devon.[46] The shortages of the 1590s were probably more severe than those which occurred during the reigns of James I or Charles I. In 1596 the Barnstaple town clerk wrote that 'little cometh to the market and such snatching and catching for that little and such a cry that the like was never heard' and that year the mayor raised £1200 to purchase a ship's load of grain to be delivered solely for the town's residents because they could 'not have corn for money'. In June 1597 three local ships arrived with rye from Danzig.[47] The officials at Plymouth also bought grain from Danzig.[48] The price of corn remained high into the summer because of continuing wet weather.

Harvests appear to have been satisfactory until 1606 when the winters of 1606-1607 and 1607-1608, were extremely cold ('as the like were never seen'), and the lead pipes in Plymouth froze.[49] Because of the cold there was a suspicion in the spring of 1608 that the wheat had died in the ground and farmers re-planted barley in its place. However deficient the crop may have been, 'very unseasonable' wet weather further diminished the harvest. Consequently there was a shortage of corn and prices did not diminish with the harvest but increased.[50] In May 1608 three Cornish justices at St Austell had written to the justices of Portsmouth for supplies of corn because of high prices caused by a local scarcity in what was called 'the western parts'. This could have meant all of Cornwall. The justices hoped that there was surplus grain in Hampshire. Shortly afterwards 100 quarters of barley was arranged to be transported to Mevagissey 'for the relief of the poor fishermen there... or to the poor inhabitants of any other [Cornish] town'.[51] In total 2,736 bushels of wheat were imported into Mount's Bay between the spring of 1608 and the summer of 1609. In the spring of 1608 corn arrived from Ireland and later in the year from Dover, Chichester, Portsmouth, Southampton and Weymouth. Whereas initially imports were of wheat, oatmeal, barley and some rye, by January it was increasingly dominated by malt, including oaten malt, although considerable quantities of grain were still being imported. It appears as though the market was saturated by 27 July 1609 when the *Edward* of Dover brought in 130 quarters of malt but sold only sixty bushels. Similarly, on 3 August the *Peter of Sandwich* left with its 120 quarters of malt unsold.[52]

In November 1608 the Mayor of Exeter negotiated with a local merchant for the delivery within 3 to 6 months of 4,000 bushels of French rye for the city's poor.[53] In October 1608 the Devon justices had noted that dearth had increased the price of victuals and that some prisoners at the gaol had 'perished through want'. The justices ordered that sufficient corn should be brought into the markets and in October 1609 restrained malt-making in order that barley should be used for baking bread. The harvest in 1609 was affected by a wet August and the Devon justices wrote to the Privy Council that all types of grain were already expensive and would further increase in price unless there were imports from other counties.[54]

It appears as though the corn harvests in Cornwall and Devon were sufficient for the following 13 years until 1622. Indeed, the harvest of 1620 was said to have been one of the best ever known. However, the following year the weather was so cold and wet that the harvest was not fully brought in until October. Then, in 1622, one particular storm was blamed for having spoiled the crop. Shortly before sunset on 18 August one Faythfull Fotherstone, a dyer, left Boyton parish church, on the border between Cornwall and Devon, and travelled north-westwards (presumably along the river Ottery) towards his home in St Gennys, some 10 miles away. He reached the parish of North Petherwin 'about an [sic] hour in the night' when 'extreme' and 'vehement' weather drove him to seek shelter in the doorway of a stranger's cottage.[55] The storm must have quickly passed to Colyton in east Devon because Sir Walter Yonge noted that on

> the 19th of August 1622 being Monday [at] about one of the clock in the morning, the wind arose and blew so vehemently for six hours, that it brake down divers strong trees. It quealed all hedges towards the south that they davered [withered] as if they had been scorched with lightning. It spoiled standing corn so, as in many places it seemed that all the corn (especially barley and oats) had been threshed or beaten out of the husks. By report there is £200 loss and hurt done to corn in Axmouth only by the said wind.

William Whiteway made similar notes in his diary and he also recorded that the 'exceeding' storm that day had caused the shipwreck of seven ships en route from La Rochelle to Plymouth. The storm must have been only one contributing factor to a disappointing harvest.[56] In contrast, for the rest of the country it was said that the weather had been wet during the summer and had then improved. This was claimed to have been the cause for the mildew and 'blasting' which ruined the crop nationally.[57] Whatever the explanation, on 4 October 1622 the Devon justices ordered the suppression of unlawful malting and then only three months later decided that no barley was to be purchased for malt-making.[58] The harvest failure coincided with the national depression of the early 1620s which, because of a general loss of earnings, increased the difficulties caused by high corn prices in 1622.

In 1623 wet weather again diminished the harvest yield. In June a ship's cargo of rye, which had been confiscated at Tor Bay, was ordered to be sold locally because of the scarcity of corn there, and in December 1623 the Privy Council noted that in the 'western parts' the price of grain had remained high.[59] There were sufficient harvests between 1623 and 1630, though there were concerns in 1626 and especially in 1627. Walter Yonge noted that in 1626 the weather was at first wet and unseasonable, which ruined corn and hay, but later conditions suddenly changed and there appears to have been a good harvest; Whiteway also noted unfavourable weather and attributed the miraculous change in weather, and the good harvest, to the intervention of the King who had proclaimed a general fast. Whiteway noted that little rain had fallen from the following February through to June but the remainder of 1627 was very wet. Alexander Daniel, of Tresilian in the parish of Newlyn East in Pydar hundred, also noted in his diary that the wheat harvest had 'much failed through the excessive rain which fell this last precedent winter [of 1627 to 1628], continuing near a quarter of a year together, which washed it out of the ground'.[60] The summer of 1629 was dry but the following winter was very wet but not cold. Whiteway noted that the price of corn began to rise as early as April 1630 and continued to do so until the following spring.[61] On 8 October 1629 the Devon justices had expressed concern about the 'buying, forestalling, engrossing and regrating' of a number of commodities, including malt, and also ordered the suppression of the 'excessive making of malt whereby the price of corn is like greatly to increase'. In July 1630 the Devon justices again limited the amount of malt-making and then on 5 October gave further orders because of a dearth of corn. Three days later ten orders were sent out for the justices; among these were that constables were required to take note of malt making and there was a restraint of the export of all corn-meal and biscuit except that which was to provision English ships. The justices were ordered to enquire from the petty constables what the quantity of spare grain was and how many corn masters and sellers there were in their parishes. Six months later, on 15 April 1631, the constables were required to oversee the selling of corn at their markets. Firstly, the market bells were to be rung twice, with the second ringing at least an hour after the first. Secondly, no badger or carrier of corn was to be allowed in the market after the second ringing. Thirdly, no forestallers, engrossers, regraters, millers or malsters were allowed in the market at any time. Finally, any unsold corn was to remain at the market to be sold the following market day. The following week the justices also ordered that corn was to be brought weekly into each market and that the poor were to be given preference at the market.[62]

At the beginning of 1630 corn was exported from Cornwall in considerable quantities, not only to nearby Plymouth but also to Dorchester and Bristol. Throughout the spring of 1630 considerable amounts of malt and barley, and some wheat and peas, were also imported into Plymouth, as they had been in 1608, from such ports along the Channel as Chichester, Portsmouth, Dover and Shoreham. Grain imports declined through the summer months, presumably as shortages occurred in south-east England. However, from 29 November onwards substantial amounts of grain were again brought into Plymouth from such Cornish ports as Fowey, Truro, Penryn, Helston and Padstow. Exports from Chichester and Portsmouth resumed with the harvest of 1631.[63] As will be seen below, the quantity of Cornish grain which was exported does not indicate a sufficient harvest, but rather the result of the opportunities presented to corn merchants by victuallers.

The harvest of 1631 appears to have been sufficient for local needs although on 4 October the Devon justices ordered, because of concern throughout the country, that all maltsters were to be restrained from buying barley and making malt except those who provisioned ships. However, that winter individual licenses were granted for the making of limited amounts of malt which may indicate that local supplies were sufficient. Certainly the justices' certificates indicate a reasonable, if not good, harvest. In May 1633 the justices in their divisions were required to oversee the suppression of malt-making according to the 'rising and falling of corn',[64] and then in July, malt-makers were restrained for a further year. There was a drought from spring through to Christmas 1634 and the Devon justices limited malt-making in 1634 and 1635. They were again alarmed about the effects of the 'extraordinary dry spring' of 1636, which ruined the barley crop, and restricted the use of barley because of concern for the poor.[65]

In 1622 and again in 1630 the corn harvest in Cornwall (and Devon) was most probably at best indifferent. The evidence points to shortages as well as surpluses. While the justices of Trigg and Lesnewth had stressed in January 1631 that there was not sufficient 'to suffice the persons which buy their corn' (69,70) the High Sheriff wrote a month later that Cornwall was 'as well stored with corn as in any former years'. Undoubtedly the harvest yield varied across the two counties. For example, it is curious that there was also a report of insufficient grain in 1630 from east Devon where reportedly there was a 'great complaint among the poor that they can not get corn for money'.(64) East Devon should have been one of the more stable grain-producing areas as compared with two areas which were more vulnerable to poor harvests and subsequent corn shortages: these were the far west of Cornwall and an area stretching from the Upper Tamar valley through into north Devon.

There is evidence that the Penwith peninsula was short of corn in 1608, 1622 and again in 1630. The justices of Lesnewth, Trigg, Kerrier and Penwith all reported in their certificates of 1623 that 'there is great want of corn... it is feared that the price will daily increase'. Their claims are made somewhat suspicious by the fact that their certificates were almost exact duplicates. Only that of Penwith differed: there was the codicil that prices would increase 'if foreign parts help us not'.(45-7) At St Ives in 1630 prices were also high and stocks were low[66] while from Penryn had come the warning in 1608 that there were not sufficient supplies of corn in the markets and that the urban populations would 'perish'.(82) The vulnerability must have reflected the comparatively low amount of good farmland in the peninsula.

As noted below, Dr Paul Slack has suggested that northern Devon was more susceptible to disease than other parts of the county because of the poorer makeup of the region. It had higher rainfall, poorer soil and was much less wealthy than south Devon.[67] Certainly it was claimed in 1630 that the hundreds on the western side of Dartmoor could 'hardly endure one bad year'.(77) Again, as with west Cornwall, there were probably not the large supplies of corn held over from preceding harvests that were needed during harvest failures. These two areas were probably vulnerable because during general corn shortages neighbouring areas were unable to supplement their deficient harvests.

CORN PRICES

Professor W.G. Hoskins' analysis of the annual corn prices at Exeter has shown the wide range of fluctuations caused by the quality of harvests.[68]Prices were very local and reflected a complex range of influences including the substitution of other grains and pulses for wheat. According to Carew, who must have been thinking of the recent shortages in the 1590s, one notable benefit of the increased popularity of barley growing was that when the price of wheat was high the poor had been able to use the surplus barley as a substitute grain for baking their bread. Curiously, no mention was made in the Pydar survey of bakers using any grain other than wheat for their bread,[69] although at Exeter in 1630 the county justices were concerned about the price of barley which they noted the poor used for baking bread.[70] The Pydar survey recorded that in that hundred there were 25 bakers who weekly needed a total of 46½ bushels of wheat. Both Padstow and St Columb Major had five bakers each and the bakers in the latter used a total of 18 bushels a week. Of course many, particularly those in farmhouses, would have produced their own bread, whether of wheat or barley, but there was still a need for bakers who sold bread to those who did not have the means to produce their own.

One difficulty with assessing corn prices is the considerable difference between markets in the measure of a bushel. The Winchester measure, six gallons to a bushel, does not appear to have been adhered to in Cornwall or Devon. Carew recognized that there was a great difference in the measure of a bushel between Cornish markets:

the land measure differeth in divers places, from eighteen to twentyfour gallons the bushel, being least in the eastern parts and increasing to the westward where they measure oats by the hogshead.[71]

When writing to the Privy Council about the prices of corn Sir John Roe, former High Sheriff of Cornwall, described them, as his successor did a few weeks later, in gallons and not bushels because 'the measure of the bushel in this county is uncertain'.(58,60) By the 1620s it appears that the measures which

Carew knew had changed somewhat: the measure was 20 gallons of wheat to a bushel in the hundreds of Kerrier, Pydar and Trigg,(**82,57,70**) and at Launceston it was 16 gallons.(**1,71**) In Devon there was a wider spectrum: in several places it was 12 gallons,(**9,86**) in north-west Devon it was 'nearer about 12 gallons',(**51**) at Newton Abbot it was 13(**75**) and only 10 at Crediton and Exeter.(**7,8,81**) The justices of East Devon claimed to have the smallest bushel; in some markets it was 10 and in others only 9.(**74**) There were also differences between the types of grain; in Lesnewth hundred a bushel of oats was 20 gallons, four more than that of wheat and barley(**69**) while in south Devon it was a peck larger than that of wheat and barley;(**9**) at Dartmouth a bushel of wheat was half larger than barley.(**62**) Finally, when grain was transported to Plymouth from Helston, Truro, Fowey and Padstow it was rated at 20 gallons to the bushel.[72]

Table 3
PRICES OF A GALLON OF CORN IN PENCE IN CORNWALL AND DEVON

1623

date	wheat	barley	oats	rye
25 January	9.0			
7 February	8.4	4.8	2.2	6.6
14 February	7.5			
15 February	9.2	4.8		6.4
22 February	8.0	5.0	2.5	6.0
27 February	8.25	5.25	2.+	6.75
28 February	9.5			7.3
13 March	9.0	5.6	2.25	
13 March	9.0	5.6	2.25	
15 March	9.0	5.6		7.2
1 April	9.0	5.2	5.75	
11 April	9.0		2.0	7.0
24 April	10.8	6.0		7.2

Source:(2,7,1,8-10,42,45-6,43,47,49,50)

1631

date	wheat	barley	oats	rye
c. 1 January	9.0			
28 January	6.9	4.2	2.6	5.4
28 January	8.1	5.4	2.4	6.0
5 February	9.0	5.0	2.5	
8 February	7.5			
1 May	7.0			
4 June	8.25			
23 November	6.92			
24 November	9.3	6.0	5.0	

Source:(59,69-70,60,71,65,73,75-6)

Table 3 shows the uneven nature of corn prices but it disguises the local nature of the differences: the rates differed enormously from one part of the region to another. Prices were also more complicated than the table suggests: there were different qualities of each grain whereby 'best' corn commanded a higher charge.(9,75)[73] Prices in 1623 were high but were probably not as high as in 1608: at Penryn in October of that year a gallon of wheat cost between 7 and 8d but it was suggested that by the following Easter it would have risen to 12d.(82) At Exeter in October a gallon of wheat cost 12d.[74] The greatest escallation of prices seems to have occurred at Barnstaple in 1597 when the harvest was 'disastrous' in the West Country: a bushel of wheat was then sold at 20s in stark contrast to only 4s a year later.[75] In general, prices peaked in late spring or early summer but occasionally inclement weather kept the rates high throughout the year.

Although the prices in Table 3 may appear to be fairly definitive it is not certain how widely these rates were actually paid as not all purchases were made at markets. As noted above, the officials of Barnstaple, Exeter and Plymouth all obtained corn for the poor and sold it at reasonable prices.[76] Likewise, the Mayor of Dartmouth wrote in 1623 that he would 'endeavour that the poorer sort may be relieved and provided for'.(2) Certainly there was great pressure by the government for the poor to be accommodated. Also, some millers sold small amounts to the poor: for example, in 1623 a miller of Moreleigh in the South Hams provided grain by pecks and half pecks to the poor.(20) Corn could also be sold on a private basis by individual farmers. Charity was also a great factor, but little is actually known about how widely neighbourly assistance was given during dearth.[77] Corn was provided in several markets 'somewhat under' the market price (8,43), but it is uncertain how widely this was done on an individual basis.

It was also claimed by several justices that high prices and scarcities were stimulated by the measures taken by the government to combat expected dearth: in 1587 when the *Book of Orders* was implemented in Barnstaple it was noted that 'many stand in doubt... they fear this order may make it dearer as it did last year'[78] and in 1630 the former and current Sheriff of Cornwall wrote that corn prices were rising more because of 'the report of the scarcity of corn in other parts of this kingdom than for any want in this county'.(58,60) The justices of Trigg and Lesnewth hundreds wrote in 1631 that they suspected that the price of corn was increasing because their survey had made it generally known that there were shortages.(70-1) Clearly the expectation of shortages increased prices: the justices in the hundreds west of Dartmoor wrote in 1631 that there was no reason for the high prices

other than an ignorant fear in the common people in general that the scarcity was much greater than indeed it was in these parts as was soon after discovered by the good plenty brought into the markets, whereupon the price was well abated before harvest'.(77)

Although two Cornish justices claimed in November 1630 that 'the cry of the poor is so lamentable, as it will grieve any man to hear it',(**52**) the shortages may not have been as severe as they suggested: in the government's opinion the shortages were worse in other parts of the country and it subsequently allowed considerable amounts of Cornish grain to be transported out of the county.

DEARTH AND THE FISHERIES

The full impact of harvest failure in the South West was both cushioned and increased by the widespread involvement in fishing. Both Carew in 1602 and his friend John Hooker at about the same time noted that pilchards had traditionally been a considerable source of inexpensive food for the poor, but that greater exports, particularly to the continent, had made fish not only more expensive, but difficult to obtain. A scarcity of pilchards in 1594, which coincided with high corn prices, reportedly put 'the common people in great distress' and in 1633, again during harvest difficulties, the county justices were concerned when reports reached them that fish was 'not to be had as the law provided'. Their concern lay with sufficient supplies being available to the poor at reasonable prices.[79] In 1630 Thomas Westcote had noted in *A View of Devonshire* that fish 'eased the price of victuals in the market'.[80] Carew noted that the poor used shellfish to save them 'from dread of starving, for every day they may gather sufficient to preserve their life, though not to please their appetites'.[81] Fish was acquired in various ways. Some went directly to buy fish: in 1584 Robert Peers of South Huish near Salcombe in Devon testified that he usually proceeded once a month to the seaside to buy fish from the fishermen's boats for his own provision,[82] and in 1632 two husbandmen of Farway in East Devon rode five miles to Seaton only in order to purchase fish.[83] For many inhabitants of inland parishes jowters (or fish-hawkers), such as John Lyle of East Teignmouth in 1614, provided them with fish; in Colaton Raleigh one lane leading from the shore was called the 'jowters way'.[84] Certain places were known for providing the surrounding area with cheap food: for instance, the hinterland of St Ives was noted as being dependent on its fish for food.[85] Tristram Risdon noted in his *Survey of Devon* that Sidmouth was 'one of the especialist fisher towns of this shire and serveth much provision into the east parts' and from Teignmouth 'the county is from thence plentifully served'.[86]

However, during times of corn shortages the region's interest in fishing had a detrimental effect on local grain supplies. The South West had developed, from the early sixteenth century, an increasing interest in the fisheries of the North West Atlantic, particularly those of Newfoundland. Victualling the fleet, which in 1604 was said to number some 150 westcountry vessels each year,[87] no doubt stimulated corn production throughout the South West but also made great demands. In 1622 Richard Whitbourne of Exmouth estimated the victualling costs of a Newfoundland ship carrying a crew of 40 seamen. It needed 11,000 hundred weight of biscuit bread, 26 tons of beer and cider,

4 hogsheads of beef, 10 fat hogs, 30 bushels of peas, 2 barrels of oatmeal, 2 firkins of butter and 2 hundred weight of cheese.[88] This was not an idle estimate: in 1610 John Rashleigh of Fowey victualled the *Success* of Fowey, carrying a crew of 37, with 9,300 hundred weight of biscuit, 24 tons of beer, 3 hogsheads of beef, 1 hogshead of pork, 2 flitches of bacon, 2 gallons of mustard seed and 4 hogsheads of peas.[89]

While in times of plenty victualling could be viewed as a valuable activity, in other circumstances it became a cause of some concern. In 1608 the Cornish justices reported that because a Barnstaple brewer had bought more than 700 bushels of corn for the making of bread and beer for the Newfoundland fleet there were local shortages.[90] On 9 November 1630 several justices of east Cornwall complained that Plymouth brewers were buying Cornish grain to the detriment of the local supplies of corn.(52-5) The survey of Pydar shows that in the autumn of 1630 merchants not only from nearby Truro but from Saltash, Bideford, Bristol and Dorchester were buying corn. This included Abraham Jennings, a merchant who was heavily involved in the Newfoundland and New England fisheries, and also George Way of Dorchester who was similarly involved in the latter fisheries. Curiously, Jennings was noted on the survey as being a resident in Cornwall (at Saltash on the Tamar),(57) but he actually resided in nearby Plymouth.[91] George Way purchased 40 bushels of wheat from one Padstow man, and, together with Jennings, purchased a further 30 bushels. Later, Way petitioned the Privy Council to allow him to again purchase Cornish grain for his New England voyages. George Shurt of Bideford, another merchant involved in overseas fishing, also bought corn from Padstow.(57)

Two Plymouth brewers who were examined before the Cornish justices on 3 November were required to present their case on 20 November before the Privy Council. In a petition they contended that they regularly supplied the Royal Navy, as well as the fishing fleets, with bread and beer and would be unable to continue that service without the Cornish grain.(52-5) The government may well have viewed the petition favourably because of the recent wars with Spain and France in which Plymouth had played an important part as a victualling port: on 26 November the Privy Council instructed the Lord Treasurer to allow the petitioners to export grain from Cornwall, and only three days later one of the brewers resumed exports of Cornish grain to Plymouth. Between 29 November 1630 and 30 March 1631 he exported from Fowey 7 shiploads of wheat, barley and oats, chartering three Fowey vessels, the *Rose*, the *Thomas* and the *Grace*. These vessels were also used by other merchants, including the fore-mentioned Abraham Jennings and his brother Ambrose, but other ships also brought Cornish grain, biscuit bread and malt from ports along the entire south Cornish coast.

Padstow appears to have regularly furnished corn for the Bristol merchants, although they were principally supplied from their own hinterland. The *Trinity* of Padstow sailed regularly to Bristol bringing corn, and some tin, and returned with such commodities as iron, soap, tar and hops. Between 24 October 1629 and 24 September 1630 the port exported 1,000 bushels of wheat to Bristol. Other local ships which were involved were the *Anne* and the *Elizabeth*, both of Padstow, the *Francis* and the *John*, both of Port Issac, and the *Willing Mind* of Boscastle. The *Speedwell* of Padstow also brought 300 bushels of beans, possibly not locally grown, to Bristol. Ships of other ports also exported grain from Padstow, most notably there were the *Francis* and the *William* of Northam which on 4 November 1629 brought 350 bushels of wheat to Bideford and the *Marie* of Braunton which in May and July 1629 sailed with 600 bushels of oats and 60 bushels of wheat for Barnstaple.[92]

The draining of local corn supplies for the overseas fisheries was a problem not confined to Cornwall. At Bristol in 1630 merchants were also depleting local stocks of corn for their fishing voyages to Newfoundland.[93] In 1633 fifteen Barnstaple merchants were forced to agree to provide for their own shipping needs more than 550 bushels of corn from outside sources in order to prevent a local shortage.[94]

The development of colonial emigration, as distinct from the South West's traditional fishery migration, also created demands for victuals. In the spring of 1630 more than a thousand colonists left England for New England. The *Amity* of Lyme Regis was one vessel involved: it left Plymouth on 7 March with 38 hogsheads and 32 barrels 'filled with peas, beef, pork, butter, cheese, bread and other provisions'.[95] More significantly for Cornwall and Devon, the fisheries also played a key role in the development of colonization. While the migration of fishermen to the overseas fisheries had been a routine phenomenon there were other opportunities. For example, in Newfoundland fishermen were being hired to 'over-winter' at the fishing stations. Moreover, with the development of the fishery at northern New England it was profitable to hire men to remain at the 'plantations' for several years. During the early seventeenth century Robert Trelawny, a merchant of Plymouth, hired many hundreds of fishermen, mostly from south-west Devon and south-east Cornwall, for his station at Richmond Island off the Maine coast. These seamen included apprentices who, while working at the island for three years, had their wages paid directly to their masters in the Plymouth area.[96] It was not just the migratory fishery that required provisioning: the development of permanent fishing settlements also needed victuals, at least initially. In 1630 Trelawny sent corn-meal from Looe to the fishing plantation. But while his manager, John Winter of Holberton in south Devon, had previously also required pork he was soon asking that no more be sent because the station had become self-sufficient.[97]

ALEHOUSES AND THE MALTING OF BARLEY

Included amongst the directions given in the *Book of Orders* on dearth were instructions to control alehouses. The state's intention was to limit the amount of barley which was used for the making of ale and beer by limiting the use of barley and also suppressing what was regarded as an excess of alehouses.[98] In 1623, and again in 1630, the justices of Cornwall and Devon responded to the wishes of the Privy Council that alehouses be controlled. The boroughs of Launceston, Dartmouth, Exeter, Plymouth and Barnstaple sent reports in February 1623 in which the officials emphasized their compliance with the orders and reiterated their reform of any making of strong beer.(1-5) The Mayor of Exeter wrote that they had reduced the number of alehouses to a 'competent number... for the necessary use of travellers and of the inhabitants of this city'.(3) The mayor of Dartmouth reported that they

> have suppressed so many of them as conveniently we might, respecting the
> number of the poorer sort of the inhabitants who are not able to make
> provision for themselves and the daily resort hither of strangers by sea...(2)

In the certificates of the justices there are also references to their restricting alehouses: the justices in north-west Devon wrote in 1623 that the rural 'tipplers' (retailers of ale and other intoxicating drinks) had ceased their trade because of their poverty, but they indicated that this was not the case in the towns.(51)

However, alehouse restrictions were a common occurrence, even when harvests were good, largely because alehouses were the focus for leisure activities, but also for other reasons. In the late 1620s some restrictions on alehouses in Devon were initiated because of concern over the spread of plague.[99] Many restrictions were made for moral considerations: for example, in 1617 the Devon justices ordered that 'any wife in the absence of her husband being either at sea or in any trade of fishing or otherwise being absent and being forbidden by her said husband from brewing or selling of ale without license' was to be sent to a house of correction.[100] There was continual concern over the large number of drinking establishments, whether those which had official sanction or the many which sold intoxicating drinks illegally.

At the beginning of the seventeenth century Cornwall was, according to Carew, poorly provided with alehouses and inns. In 1577 a national survey had been ordered of the number of alehouses and the returns survive for the hundreds of Pydar, Penwith, Powder and Kerrier. They show that there were 30 wine taverns and 132 alehouses[101] whereas a similar report for Devon recorded there were 80 inns, 40 wine taverns and 400 alehouses.[102] More than fifty years later the Pydar survey recorded the names of tipplers and malsters; there were 11 malsters who converted a total of 31 bushels of barley into malt each week and there were also 53 tipplers who brewed 78½ bushels of malt weekly. Padstow was clearly a centre for malting and brewing: it had 3 resident malsters and there were 13 tipplers who brewed some 31 bushels of malt each week.(57) Doubtless there was strong demand in local alehouses in the port for beer and ale by residents and strangers as well as by ship's victuallers. But St Columb Major was also important: it had 4 malsters who used 24 bushels of barley weekly and there were 19 tipplers who needed 19 bushels of malt each week. On 16 March 1631 the Assize judges noted that three of these malsters of St Columb Major had persisted with the malting of barley 'in contempt' of an earlier order. The justices later relented and allowed the men to continue malting because of the considerable amount of grain brought to the town only by the three men. Two local justices, one of whom was John Prideaux (one of the signatories to the Pydar survey), were asked to consider whether the men should continue to use barley or oats for their malting.[103]

Barley was not the only grain used for the making of malt. Carew wrote that within recent memory Cornish husbandmen had drunk only water 'or at best whey' and that no barley had been used for malt but only oats.[104] Oaten malt was still in use in Cornwall and Devon, but it was not much liked. John Hooker wrote that oats were 'spoiled' on the reaches of northern Dartmoor. Consequently, they could be used for producing meal but not for making drink for either 'man, horse or hog' because 'It will make him to vomit and for the time very sick. Notwithstanding, the people of that country being used thereat do endure the same very well.'[105]

Although the restrictions on the making and selling of ale and beer must have created many difficulties there were also opportunities for others: for those in areas which had apple orchards any failures with corn harvests must have enhanced the price of cider.

DISEASE AND TRAVELLERS

There was a fear that disease occurred after dearth: when issuing orders to rectify the harvest failure in 1630 the Privy Council referred to 'famine and the diseases which follow the want of wholesome food'.[106] In Cornwall and Devon, as in the rest of the country, there were many outbreaks of infectious disease but was there any association between them and harvest failure?

It is seldom certain whether smallpox, measles, tuberculosis, whooping cough, typhus or bubonic plague caused an increase in deaths. Carew commented that Cornish houses were 'most pestered' with rats but it is not apparent that the county suffered unduly from plague. He also suggested that Bodmin should have been better called 'Badham' because it was the most 'contagiously' sited place in Cornwall ('every general infection is here first admitted and last excluded')[107] but Bodmin was one of many places to experience disease. There is much evidence in parish records of disease in the years immediately preceding our period; for example there was a considerable increase in burials in the parish of Breage near Helston in 1578 and at St Columb Minor there was almost a ten-fold increase in deaths during an outbreak of plague which occurred during 1591-2. Disease during the Civil War spread as far west as St Just-in-Penwith.[108]

More is known about the incidence of disease for Devon than for Cornwall because of the survival of Devon Quarter Sessions records and examination of this pattern reveals some similarities to that of Cornwall and the relationship to harvest failure.

Bubonic plague and viral infections were responsible for mortality crises in some part of Devon at least once, on average, every decade from 1540 to 1650. Their occurrence could be very specific to a locality. There were at least five outbreaks of plague in early Stuart Devon: in Dartmouth and Plymouth in 1602, in Otterton and Axminster in 1611 and 1612, throughout Devon from 1625 to 1628, in several parishes in 1636 to 1637 and again throughout the county during the Civil War between 1642 and 1646. There was also infectious disease at Ilfracombe in 1602, at Exeter, Barnstaple and Great Torrington in 1604, at Kingswear in 1604 and 1605, at Tormohun in 1611 and within the county generally in 1640.[109]

However, Dr Paul Slack has shown that there was a contrary association between disease and dearth conditions in Devon, and that there was a difference in epidemic experience between the northern and southern coasts, divided as it was by Dartmoor. He suggests that this was partly the result of the differences between their corn-producing capabilities: the north was a poorer producer than the south which was also in a better position for importing foreign grain in times of scarcity. But southern Devon was more open to plague because of its greater access to outside shipping. The warmer climate of south Devon also helped to breed the plague flea; overall south Devon had a greater plague mortality. North Devon's more isolated position not only reduced the risks of exposure to infectious disease, but also inhibited the importing of corn in dearth, opening the region to periodic problems of malnutrition.

From 1622 to 1623 there was an increased number of burials in Colyton and also at Barnstaple, where some six per cent of the population died. Nearby, at Bideford, there was an outbreak of typhus, a disease associated with malnutrition. There was also an increase in the number of burials at St Budeaux outside Plymouth in 1622, but the increase began before the harvest failure, suggesting that corn shortages could at most have enhanced the mortality rate.[110] However, the topography of Cornwall is markedly different from that of Devon and it is unlikely that many deaths were directly caused by malnutrition in 1623 or 1630; if this had occurred it should have been noted in the Justices' certificates.

However, there was disease in Cornwall in the years between the harvest failures of 1622 and 1630 which were obliquely caused by food shortages but not harvest failure. Although there was a national outbreak of plague in 1625, disease in Cornwall was that year linked to Plymouth's use as a naval base during the wars of the late 1620s. Plague, and probably several other diseases, spread quickly in 1625 through the concentration of sailors and soldiers temporarily stationed there, many of whom were poorly fed and housed. The authorities were rapidly unable to provide food and housing for the several thousand pressed men and billeted them into the surrounding parishes of Devon and Cornwall. There was apprehension that this would spread disease, and indeed there were 'sick' soldiers who died whilst at Liskeard in 1626. The parish church was used to house the men, and the town's fair, held on 24 June, was cancelled in 1626 and 1627. The borough paid one shilling to have the church cleaned after the soldiers left, and also bought two books of thanksgiving for the 'staying' of the plague.[111] There was also 'sickness' at Saltash,[112] as well as at Falmouth 'and other places'.[113]

A sharp increase of travellers during dearth was viewed seriously, partly because it was feared that it could help spread infection. In some cases disease arrived in the South West because of the long coastline. Certainly the borough officials at St Ives were worried in 1603 about plague arriving either by land or sea and in 1629-30 they refused to allow the crew of an Irish vessel, which had arrived from France, to come ashore because of 'the sickness' aboard.[114] In 1589 disease had been brought into Exeter through captured Portuguese prisoners.[115] It was the arrival of strangers, particularly those from places which were known to have disease, which caused the greatest alarm. The appearance around midnight in early September 1625 of the corpse of a Crediton weaver in the town-place at Okehampton raised such concern. William Rowdon, a labourer also of Crediton, had been paid to bring the weaver on horseback from Crediton (presumably by someone trying to avoid infection) and admitted that the weaver had 'some dangerous or infectious disease'.[116] Whether Rowdon was responsible or not, there was plague at Okehampton shortly afterwards.[117] The movement of grain supplies in years of dearth may also have assisted the spread of disease.[118]

There were extraordinary factors which caused an increase in the number of travellers at this time. Not only were there a considerable number of impressed men travelling to and from Plymouth, but there was an increase in the number of travellers (or vagrants) in the South West caused by the national depression in 1621. However, in the South West the principal migration of vagabonds, or travellers, was west to east, towards London.119 For example, one such transient was Phillipa Arter, a spinster of St Columb Minor, who testified in July 1637 that after she travelled to Plymouth (and spent all her money there) she had slept, together with 'divers others both Irish and English', in an 'outhouse' belonging to one Mr Trelawny. This was presumably Robert Trelawny, merchant and M.P. for Parliament who resided at Ham, just outside Plymouth, but who also had a town-house in Plymouth.[120]

Indigenous movement from Cornwall eastwards into Devon should not have introduced disease into Cornwall.[121] However, there was also longstanding migration from further afield in the form of Irish travellers of whom Carew wrote:

few shires can show more, or own fewer, than Cornwall. Ireland prescribeth to be the nursery, which sendeth over yearly, yea and daily, whole shiploads of these crooked slips.[122]

In 1629 the Devon justices noted that the county 'swarmed' with Irish 'rogues'.[123] Few churchwarden accounts do not have references to the giving of money to Irish travellers and the majority of vagrants in Devon were Irish, with the Cornish being the second highest group.[124]However, while much of this migration was probably due to longstanding economic causes some Irish arrived in 1630 as a result of an Irish harvest failure.[125] Notwithstanding, there is no evidence that they spread disease.

The variety and sheer number of strangers travelling through the South West remained a problem throughout the 1630s, increasing the difficulties posed by periodic corn scarcity and infectious disease. While there was disease in Cornwall and Devon around 1622 and 1630, harvest failures in the South West were not the direct cause, although migration created by economic disruption in other areas may have assisted its movement.

CONCLUSION

Harvest failure in early Stuart Cornwall and Devon was generally due to unfavourable weather, whether it was a cold and wet winter or a wet summer before harvest. It is widely accepted that wheat and barley were the predominant grains, in contrast to a greater use of oats in northern England, but it is less certain whether there were many other significant differences between Cornwall, Devon and other parts of England. As grain formed a considerable part of the general diet during corn shortages there must have been an increased reliance on other food sources. Doubtless there were attempts to obtain more vegetables and herbs but it is not known how widely available these were to those without a small-holding nor do we know how vibrant the complementary wild food economy was: did the foodstuffs of the countryside, plant and animal, provide a strong buffer against famine?

Examination of Cornish harvest failure, and dearth, within a regional context reveals some striking local elements which were not factors found by Andrew Appleby in his study of Cumberland. It establishes that some of the causes were man-made and were directly related to the demands of the overseas fisheries. Cornish grain-producers were part of a large and established regional network of suppliers to the maritime victuallers. Simultaneously, the fisheries offered consumers both a protective shield to dearth (in the form of cheap protein) and a constant drain of corn stocks. It also acted as an economic stimulus to the economy in general and to grain-producers in particular. Few Cornish parishes are not within easy reach of the sea and the impact was dependent upon the nature of the fisheries in each locality. The fisheries changed drastically between each area; for example, while the fishery off Newfoundland may have been important in many parts of Devon (particularly in south Devon), it appears to have only been used in Cornwall by seamen in Fowey, Looe and the Tamar parishes. Similarly, the Irish fishery was significant to many places, but particularly so to Padstow, St Ives and Mount's Bay. Also, the inshore fisheries were very localized - most notably, pilchards on the south coast and herring generally along the north. There were also other factors, most notably fishing's seasonal nature and sudden fluctuations. We do not know what effect the fisheries had on the pattern of crisis mortality. Plague is generally known to have occurred in summer when the many thousands of seamen were fishing off Newfoundland. One can only surmise about the effect of the fisheries on individual motivation for migration, and later, emigration. Poorer families must have been more likely to send their young abroad to the fisheries during times of economic hardship but did their employment partly shield these boys and their families from the occurrence of disease, famine and poverty, both at home and at sea?

Dr R.B. Outhwaite has recently pointed out that 'one can produce lengthy catalogues of developments that may have relieved populations of the deadlier consequences of dearth. It is much more difficult, however, to attach weights to these possible causes of improvement'.[126] Irrespective of the unknown factors which assisted society with overcoming corn shortages it may perhaps be useful to be reminded of its stimulating effect during years of plenty. Carew argued regarding his paradox of dearth that:

> Their objection, who fear lest the transporting of much away will leave too
> little home, I answer with this observation: when the price of corn faileth,
> men generally give over surplus tillage, and break no more ground than will
> serve to supply their own turn... where through it falleth out, that an ill
> kerned, or saved, harvest soon emptieth their old store and leaveth them in
> necessity, to seek relief from other places. Whereas, on the other side, if
> through hope of vent they hold on their larger tillage, this retaineth one
> year's provision underhand, to fetch in another, which upon such occasion
> may easily be left at home; and of this, what Cornishman is there, that hath
> not seen the experience?[127]

In Carew's opinion Cornish insularity would have been its undoing: the optimum protection against dearth, and surest course for prosperity, lay with expansion abroad. In 1608, 1622 and 1630 it is likely that the harvest would have supplied sufficient grain for the broad population had it not been for the demands of the overseas fisheries. However, as Carew argued, those supplies were the result of encouragement given to the cultivators of new arable land. Without that motivation there would have been considerably less grain grown. Moreover, the removal of the fisheries from the general economy would have made society more vulnerable to common economic cycles of prosperity and depression. It is possible that because of this relationship and the prevailing buoyancy of the fisheries there was never any famine, although there were frequent harvest failures, and occasionally dearth.

EDITORIAL PRACTICE

The arrangement of some documents has been altered from their listing in the *Calendar of State Papers Domestic*. This has been done in order to present the documents in what is believed to have been their original sequence. Punctuation has been modernized. Abbreviations and contractions have been extended throughout except ampersands. Arabic have been substituted for Roman numerals. All Latin has been put into English and italicized. Missing words, or parts of words, caused by damage to the documents have been supplied and placed within square brackets. Christian names have for the most part been modernized, but those not generally in current use, such as Nyott, Enoder and Mawgan, have been given in their original spelling. All surnames have been printed as in the texts. Place-names also appear as in the original but modern spellings generally follow within square brackets, as do all editorial insertions.

ACKNOWLEDGEMENTS

The editor and the members of the Academic Board of the Institute of Cornish Studies would like to thank the Controller of her Majesty's Stationary Office (in respect of Crown copyright material in the Public Record Office) and the British Library for permission to publish these records.

The editor is particularly grateful to Professor Joyce Youings, Dr Jonathan Barry and Mr Tom Arkell for their comments on the text. Others who must be thanked are Dr Joan Thirsk for her advice and support, Mr Seán Goddard for producing the maps, Mrs Elizabeth Jackson and Mrs Heather Oliver for administering the subscription list, Mrs Julie Newcombe for preparing the indexes and particularly Mr Adamu Sabo who computer-typeset the editor's word-processed text. Among other individuals to whom he is indebted are Miss Angela Broome of the Royal Institution of Cornwall and Mrs Margery Rowe, Mr John Draisey and the staff of the Devon Record Office. Early research on this volume was made possible through financial support given by the Academic Board of the Institute of Cornish Studies as trustees of the Caroline Kemp scholarship fund. Finally, Paul and Sophie Ferrie must be thanked for their hospitality in London which made visits to the Public Record Office possible.

Helland, Probus   Todd Gray
May, 1992

References

1. David Arnold, *Famine, Social Crisis and Historical Change* (Oxford, 1988).
2. Andrew B. Appleby, *Famine in Tudor and Stuart England* (Liverpool,1978), 121-54; R.B. Outhwaite, *Dearth, Public Policy and Social Disturbance in England, 1550-1800* (1991), 57.
3. For its use in the period see Outhwaite, *Dearth*, 10-12.
4. Francis Lord de Dunstanville (ed.), *Carew's Survey of Cornwall* (1811), 66.
5. Appleby, *Famine in Tudor and Stuart England*, 3.
6. For farming and some discussion of harvest failure within 'Kernow' see J.Whetter, *Cornwall in the Seventeenth Century; an Economic history of Kernow* (Padstow, 1974), 21-58, 178-83.
7. Paul Slack, 'Books of Orders: the making of English Social Policy, 1577-1631', *Transactions of the Royal Historical Society*, fifth series, xxx (1980), 1-5.
8. Alan Everitt, 'The marketing of Agricultural Produce', in Joan Thirsk(ed.), *The Agrarian History of England and Wales, 1500-1640* (Cambridge, 1967) iv. 581.
9. Carew, *Survey of Cornwall*, 217.
10. I am grateful to Mrs Mary Wolffe for information supplied from her forthcoming doctoral thesis on the activities of the Devon justices, 1625-1642.
11. Slack, 'Books of Orders'. See also Anthony Fletcher, *Reform in the Provinces, the Government of Stuart England* (New Haven, 1986).
12. C[ornwall] R[ecord] O[ffice], AP/C855/1,2.
13. Todd Gray (ed.), *Early-Stuart Mariners and Shipping; the Maritime Surveys of Devon and Cornwall, 1619-35*, Devon and Cornwall Record Society, new series xxxiii (1990), 88, 90.
14. P[ublic] R[ecord] O[ffice], SP16/117/43.
15. Slack, 'Books of Orders', 12.
16. Royal Institution of Cornwall, Henderson vi, 24-5. In 1930 a church rate of St Merryn of 1642 was transcribed but it appears as though the original document has since been lost.
17. D[evon] R[ecord] O[ffice],DQS, Bundle Box 1626, Epiphany testimony 1.
18. DRO, Exeter City Court Book, 1622, f.47.
19. Carew, *Survey of Cornwall*, 63.
20. Harold Fox, 'Farming Practice and Techniques', in Edward Miller (ed.), *The Agrarian History of England and Wales* (Cambridge, 1991) iii. 303.
21. CRO, AP/B437/2.
22. Robin Stanes, *The Old Farm, A History of Farming Life in the West Country* (Devon County Council, 1990), 54.

23. Joan Thirsk, 'Farming Techniques', in Thirsk, *Agrarian History* iv. 166, 172, 173.
24. Joan Thirsk, 'The Farming Regions of England', in Thirsk, *Agrarian History* iv. 72; W.G. Hoskins, *Devon* (Newton Abbot, 1978 edn), 95, 540.
25. Carew, *Survey of Cornwall*, 61-2; PRO, SP12/88/52(iv).
26. DRO, John Hooker, *Synopsis Chorographical*, 13.
27. Thirsk, 'The Farming regions of England', 75; Hoskins, *Devon*, 93-6; Carew, *Survey of Cornwall*, 62, 89-90.
28. Donald Woodward, "An essay on manures': changing attitudes to fertilization in England, 1500-1800', in John Chartres and David Hey (eds), *English Rural Society, Essays in honour of Joan Thirsk* (Cambridge, 1990), 253-8; Fox, 'Farming Practice and Techniques', 311-14.
29. Carew, *Survey of Cornwall*, 15-17, 61-6.
30. Frank Graham (ed.), *A Topographical and Historical Description of Cornwall* (Newcastle upon Tyne, 1966), 17-18, 45; Carew, *Survey of Cornwall*, 297.
31. CRO, AP- P801/2, S910/1,2, C750/2, C390/1,2, H1047/2, W516/1,3, V97/2, D300/2, C797/1, L125/3,4; DRO, DQS Bundle Box Bapt. 1637, exam. 25.
32. Tristram Risdon, *The Chorographical Description or Survey of the county of Devon* (1811), 4.
33. Dr Williams' Library, John Quick, *Icones Sacrae Anglicanae,* 399.
34. Fox, 'Farming Practice and Techniques', 306-7.
35. Margaret Cash (ed.), *Devon Inventories*, Devon and Cornwall Record Society, new series xi (1966), 48.
36. Duchy of Cornwall Office, Dartmouth petty customs.
37. Ann Kussmaul, *Servants in Husbandry* (Cambridge, 1981), 7; Ralph A. Houlbrooke, *English Family 1450-1700* (1984); Alan Everitt, 'Farm Labourers', in Thirsk, *Agrarian History* iv. 396-465.
38. Peter Laslett, 'Size and structure of the household in England over three centuries', *Local Population Studies*, xxiii (1969), 135.
39. Nigel Goose, 'Household size and structure in early-Stuart Cambridge', *Social History*, 5 (1980), 347-85.
40. Paul Slack, *Poverty and Policy in Tudor and Stuart England*, (1988), 73-7.
41. CRO, AP- E227/2, R443/2. In 1628/9 Thomas Dungies left his property, including seven beds, to his son Sampson who reported in the following year a household of seven. Thomas Pellean, a Newlyn yeoman, had a household of eight and left in 1641 six featherbeds, two trucklebeds, and one 'other bed': CRO, AP- D300/2, P801/2.
42. See for example CRO, AP- W516/3 and for one Devon example: DRO, inventory of John Mongey of West Putford, 18 June 1602.
43. These two entries used 'have' whereas the other entires are singular households and used 'hath'.
44. The issue of household size is discussed in more depth in my forthcoming

article on the size of rural households in early Stuart Devon and Cornwall.

45. The Diary of Philip Wyot', in J.R. Chanter (ed.), *Sketches of some striking incidents in the History of Barnstaple* (Barnstaple, 1865), 91-119; *William Whiteway of Dorchester, His Diary 1618 to 1635*, Dorset Record Society (with an introduction by David Underdown), xii (1991); G. Roberts (ed.), *The Diary of Walter Yonge, Esq.*, Camden Soc., old series xli (1848).

46. DRO, DQS OB 1/1, 84, 132, 133, 137, 143, 148, 149, 153, 161, 162.

47. Wyot, *Diary*, 103-4.

48. Slack, *Plague*, 96.

49. WDRO, Widey Court Book, 1607; David B.Quinn & Aileen M. Quinn (eds), *The English New England Voyages, 1602-1608*, Hakluyt Society, 2nd series, clxi (1983), 1-7.

50. DRO, DQS, OB 1/3, f.20.

51. PRO, SP14/32/57(i). They suggested that shortages were enhanced by hoarding.

52. Whetter, *Kernow*, 182; PRO, E190/1023/5 & 6.

53. DRO, Ancient Letters, 1600-1612, 89 & ED/M/1335, L1711.

54. DRO, DQS, OB 1/3, 7, 8, 19, 20; Yonge, *Diary*, 18.

55. DRO, DQS, Bundle Box Michaelmas 1622, exam. 13; Yonge, *Diary*, 42, 52, 55; Whiteway, *Diary*, 39.

56. Yonge, *Diary*, 63; Whiteway, *Diary*, 47.

57. Thomas Birch (ed.), *Court and Times of James I* (1849) ii. 331.

58. DRO, DQS OB 1/5, 344, 362.

59. Whiteway, *Diary*, 52-3; *Acts Privy Council, 1623-1625*, 20 June and 23 December 1623.

60. Yonge, *Diary*, 94, 96; Whiteway, *Diary*, 83; P.A.S. Pool, 'The Autobiography of Alexander Daniel of Alverton', *Journal of the Royal Institution of Cornwall*, new series, vii, pt 4 (1977), 265.

61. Whiteway, *Diary*, 104, 110.

62. DRO, DQS OB 1/6, 242, 309, 339, 340.

63. PRO, E190/1032/4 & 10.

64. DRO, DQS OB 1/6, 364, 369, 374, 376, 446.

65. Whiteway, *Diary*, 142, 145, 154, 156; DRO, DQS OB 1/7, 14 July 1636.

66. John Hobson Matthews, *A History of St Ives, Lelant, Towednack and Zennor* (1892), 189.

67. Paul Slack, *The Impact of Plague in Tudor and Stuart England* (Cambridge, 1990 edn), 91-3.

68. W.G. Hoskins, 'Harvest Fluctuations and English Economic History, 1480-1619', *Agricultural History Review*, xii, pt 1 (1964), 28-46 & 'Harvest Fluctuations and English Economic History, 1620-1759', *Agricultural History Review*, xvi, pt 1 (1968), 15-31.

69. Carew, *Survey of Cornwall*, 64.

70. DRO, DQS OB 1/6, 299.

71. Carew, *Survey of Cornwall*, 146.7

72. PRO, E190/1032/4 & 10.
73. See also PRO, SP12/88/52(iii & iv). In Cornwall in 1572 best wheat was priced at 48s a quarter and second wheat at 44s.
74. DRO, DQS, OB 1/3, f.20.
75. Wyot, *Diary*, 104, 106; Hoskins, 'Price fluctuations', 46.
76. Also at Dorchester in 1630: Whiteway, *Diary*, 113.
77. John Walter, 'The social economy of dearth in early modern England', 96-128 in John Walter and Roger Schofield (eds), *Famine, disease and the social order in early modern society* (Cambridge, 1989).
78. Wyot, *Diary*, 92.
79. Carew, *Survey of Cornwall*, 104-5; Hooker, *Synopsis Chorographical*; 76; West Devon Record Office, 1082/12; A.L. Rowse, 'The dispute concerning the Plymouth pilchard fishery, 1584-91', *Economic History Review*, 7 (1932), 461-72; DRO, DQS OB 1/7, 3 October 1633.
80. Thomas Westcote, *A view of Devonshire in 1630* (1811), 375-6.
81. Carew, *Survey of Cornwall*, 104, 97.
82. DRO, Chanter 861, ff.283-4.
83. DRO, DQS bundle box 5b, Mich 1632.
84. DRO, Chanter 867, f.7; DRO, Colaton Raleigh glebe terrier.
85. Nordon, *Historical Description*, 27.
86. Risdon, *Survey of Devon*, 34, 145.
87. Gillian Cell, *English Enterprise in Newfoundland* (Toronto, 1969), 22.
88. Cell, *English Enterprise*, 151.
89. John Scantlebury, 'John Rashleigh of Fowey and the Newfoundland Cod Fishery, 1608-20', *Journal of the Royal Institution of Cornwall*, new series, viii, pt 1 (1978), 65.
90. *HMC* 9, 28 December 1608.
91. Gray, *Early Stuart Mariners and Shipping*, 81, 111.
92. PRO, E190/1136/2, 1136/4, 1031/14.
93. PRO, SP16/224/53 & 80.
94. J.R. Chanter and Thomas Wainwright (eds), *Barnstaple Records* (Barnstaple, 1900), 135.
95. Charles M. Andrews, *The Colonial Period of American History* (New Haven, 1934) i. 395; PRO, E190/1032/4. The *Supply* of Weymouth also sailed from Plymouth at this time and must have been part of the same operation: the cargo on board included 'nails, locks, hooks, twists, carpenters' tools and tools for husbandry and 16 muskets and fowling pieces'.
96. James Phinney Baxter (ed.), *The Trelawny Papers*, Maine Historical Society, new series iii (1884), 463, 31, 57-8.
97. Baxter, *Trelawny Papers*, 147.
98. S.K. Roberts, 'Alehouses, brewing, and government under the early Stuarts', *Southern History*, 45-71.
99. Roberts, 'Alehouses', 58.
100. DRO, DQS OB 1/4, Michaelmas, 1617.

101. PRO, SP12/119/2-3 cited and printed by L. Douch, *Old Cornish Inns & their place in the social history of the county* (Truro, 1966), 18, 209-11.
102. PRO, SP12/122/5(i).
103. J.S. Cockburn(ed), *Western Circuit Assize Orders* ; *a Calendar*,Camden Soc., 4th Series 17 (1976), 25, 26.
104. Carew, *Survey of Cornwall*, 183, 65.
105. Hooker, *Synopsis Chronological.*, 28-9.
106. *Acts Privy Council, 1630-1631*, 12 Sept. 1630.
107. Carew, *Survey of Cornwall*, 73, 290-1. He blamed this partly on the unhealthiness of the water conduit which ran through the churchyard. But he also thought that the fault lay with the town's plan: it was sited on one street running east to west and built onto a hillside so that 'their filth by every shower washed down through their houses into the street'.
108. CRO, parish registers of Breage, St Columb Minor and St Just parish register. I am grateful to Miss Carleen Harry & Mr David Collumb for this last reference.
109. Slack, *Plague*, 85.
110. Slack, *Plague*, 72-3, 62.
111. CRO, BLisk/280-3 & DDP.126/4/1, 136-7
112. PRO, SP16/29/46.
113. PRO, SP16/55/60. A reference to severe storms could refer to the extreme weather of October 1624: Whiteway, *Diary*, 65.
114. Matthews, *A History of St Ives*, 170-1, 189.
115. Slack, *Plague*, 85; Wyot, *Diary*, 95.
116. DRO, DQS, Bundle Box, Michaelmas, examination of William Rowdon, 14 September 1625. There had been a recent death in the household in which the weaver had recently worked.
117. PRO, SP16/30/67.
118. Slack, *Plague*, 84.
119. Paul Slack, 'Vagrants and vagrancy in England, 1598-1664', in Peter Clark and David Souden (eds), *Migration and Society in early Modern England* (1987), 62; A.L. Beier, *Masterless Men, the vagrancy problem in England 1560-1640* (1985), 34.
120. DRO, DQS, Bundle Box Bapt. 1637. Two years previously she had been whipped at Exeter for her 'roguish course of life'.
121. This may not have been the case in 1579: Slack, *Plague*, 86.
122. Carew, *Survey of Cornwall*, 184.
123. DRO, DQS OB 1/6, 25-33, 211.
124. Slack, 'Vagrants and vagrancy', 379; Beier, *Masterless Men*, 34, 62-5.
125. Beier, *Masterless Men*, 34, 63-4.
126. Outhwaite, *Dearth*, 34.
127. Carew, *Survey of Cornwall*, 66-7.

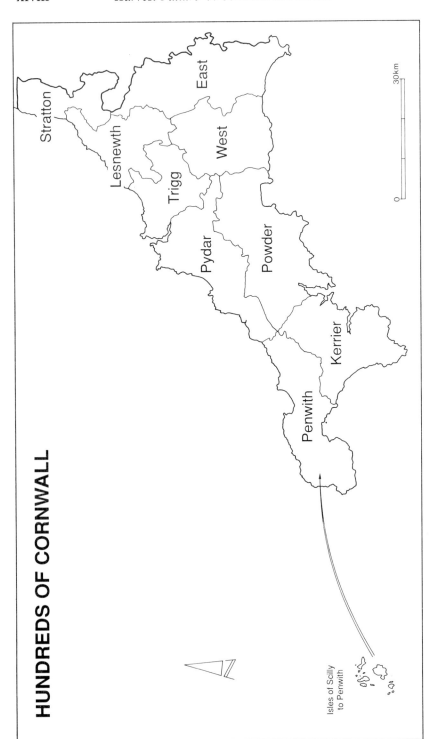

HUNDREDS OF CORNWALL

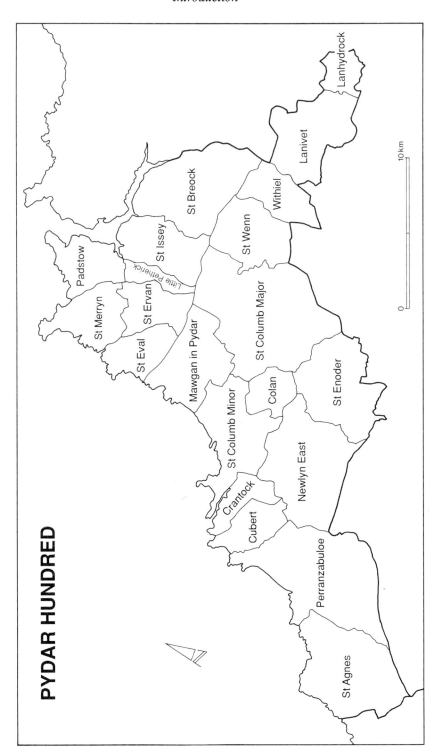

PYDAR HUNDRED

Lanhydrock

Lanivet

St Breock

Withiel

St Wenn

Padstow

St Issey

Little Petherick

St Merryn

St Ervan

St Columb Major

Mawgan in Pydar

St Eval

Colan

St Enoder

St Columb Minor

Newlyn East

Crantock

Cubert

Perranzabuloe

St Agnes

10 km

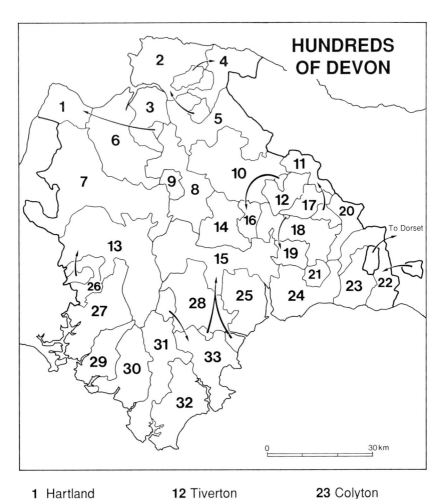

HUNDREDS OF DEVON

To Dorset

0   30 km

1 Hartland	**12** Tiverton	**23** Colyton
2 Braunton	**13** Lifton	**24** East Budleigh
3 Fremington	**14** Crediton	**25** Exminster
4 Shirwell	**15** Wonford	**26** Tavistock
5 South Molton	**16** West Budleigh	**27** Roborough
6 Shebbear	**17** Halberton	**28** Teignbridge
7 Black Torrington	**18** Hayridge	**29** Plympton
8 North Tawton	**19** Cliston	**30** Ermington
9 Winkleigh	**20** Hemyock	**31** Stanborough
10 Witheridge	**21** Ottery	**32** Coleridge
11 Bampton	**22** Axminster	**33** Haytor

STANBOROUGH AND COLERIDGE HUNDREDS

Holne

Buckfastleigh

Dean Prior

South Brent

Rattery

Dartington

Totnes

Harberton

Ashprington

North Huish

Diptford

Cornworthy

Halwell

Dittisham

Moreleigh

Loddiswell

Woodleigh

Blackawton

Stoke Fleming

Dartmouth

East Allington

Slapton

Churchstow

B

K

Sherford

Thurlestone

West
Alvington

D

Charleton

Stokenham

S. Milton

South Huish

S. Pool

Malborough

(Salcombe)

East
Portlemouth

Chivelstone

B   Buckland-tout-Saints
K   Kingsbridge
D   Dodbrooke

0   10 km

THE HARVEST FAILURE OF 1622

1. Certificate. Mayor and Burgesses of Launceston to the Privy Council, 14 February 1623.

PRO, SP14/138/34
[endorsed. To the right honourable the Lords of his Majesty's most honourable Privy Council.
14th February 1622 from *Lanceston* touching alehouses and grain.]

Right Honourable,
Our most humble duties remembered. Whereas about the five and twentieth of January last we received your Honours' letters together with a Book of Orders to us the Mayor and Burgesses of *Lannceston* in Cornwall directed to prevent the present excessive prices of corn and to suppress unnecessary alehouses whereby great quantities of barley have been vainly spent in brewing of strong beer and ale and for the performance of divers other things by the same Orders enjoined and you require a certificate of our endeavours and proceedings therein before the last of this instant of February. These are in all humility to certify unto your Honours that forthwith upon the receipt of the said letters and Orders we used our best means towards the full execution of the said Orders in every particular according to the tenor of the same, whereby we do find by experience in this short time that a bushel of wheat containing sixteen gallons, which before the receipt of the said Orders was sold in our market for twelve shillings, is now sold for ten shillings, and besides the quantity of barley brought into our market to be sold is now doubled more than it hath been heretofore which we most humbly leave to your honourable consideration. And so in all duty we rest, at your honours' service,
[signed] Richard Escott, Mayor
John Gennes Arthur Piper Hugh Vigares Henry Cary Oswald Cooke

from *Lannceston* this 14th of February 1622 [1623]

1

2. Certificate. Mayor of Dartmouth to the Privy Council, 17 February 1623.

PRO, SP14/138/40
[endorsed. To the right honourable the Lords and others of his Majesty's most honourable Privy Council.
17 February 1622. A letter from the Lord Mayor of York (sic) concerning alehouses.]

Our duties unto your Honours humbly acknowledged. According to your Honours directions by letters bearing date the last day of December last past, we have called before us all the brewers, inn holders and alehouse-keepers within this town and the liberties thereof and have suppressed so many of them as conveniently we might, respecting the number of the poorer sort of the inhabitants who are not able to make provision for themselves and the daily resort hither of strangers by sea and have also taken order that no beer be sold above the price and rate of sixteen shillings the hogshead and shall also by all lawful ways endeavour that the poorer sort may be relieved and provided for, and that there may be no unnecessary or vain consumption of corn and grain in this place hereof as by your Honours said letters it is required and as in duty we are bound, we have been bold to certify your Honours' and so do humbly cease, your honours in all duty to be commanded,
[signed] Thomas Spurwaie, Mayor   Thomas Gourney

Dartmouth the 17th of February 1622 [1623].

3. Certificate. Mayor and Aldermen of Exeter to the Privy Council, 22 February 1623.

PRO, SP14/138/62
[endorsed. To the right honourable our very good lords the Lords of his Majesty's most honourable Privy Council deliver these.
22 February 1622 certificate of alehouses from *Exon*.]

Right Honourables,
Our duties most humbly remembered to your Lordships. May it please your Honours to be advertised that upon receipt of your letters of the last of December commanding us to take course for the suppressing of the excessive number of alehouses we in performance of our duties in that service as well before the receipt of your Lordships' letters and since hath taken pains to be informed of the number of alehouses kept within this city & suburbs. ['Aswell' crossed through] And such as have set up tippling houses without license we have punished according to the statute and taken review of such as had been licensed we have suppressed some of them and have reduced them to such a

competent number as may serve (as we conceive) for the necessary use of travellers and of the inhabitants of this city and ['do' crossed through] likewise we have done our best endeavour to reform the strength of ale & beer & as far (as yet we can proceed) have reduced the same to a moderate course. Thus humbly praying your Honours to accept of this our endeavours & resolution to proceed therein to bring the same to good effect we humbly take our leave praying for the continuance of your Honours in health and prosperity we end and rest, your Honours most humbly to be commanded,
[signed] John Modyford, Mayor
Thomas Walker, Alderman John Prouse, Alderman
John Howell, Alderman Walter Borough, Alderman
Geoffrey Waltham, Alderman Ignatius Jurdain, Alderman

Exon the 22th of February 1622 [1623]

4. Certificate. Mayor and Affeerors[?] of Plymouth to the Privy Council, 24 February 1623.

PRO, SP14/138/73
[endorsed. To the right honourable the Lords of his Majesty's most honourable Privy Council, give these.
the 24th of February from *Plimmouth* about alehouses.]

Right Honourable,
Our duties in all humbleness remembered. May it please your Honours to be advertised that immediately upon the receipt of your Honours' letters we required all our alehouse-keepers to appear before us at our Guildhall and there suppressed divers such as we found either to be disorderly or which we thought to be superfluous and more then enough. And likewise have taken a strict course that in such inns and alehouses as are by us allowed the strength of beer and ale there to be sold and uttered shall be so moderated and reformed in the strength thereof that no waste shall grow thereby of the grain of the kingdom. And moreover we have taken order with our malsters and brewers that by the one no barley be wastefully spent as heretofore it hath been and with the other that their best beer which they shall brew for sale do not exceed 13s 4d the hogshead, and do purpose God willing to put such laws strictly in execution as have been formerly made for the punishment of offenders in these several kinds. Hereof we thought it our duties to acquaint your honours. And so we rest, your Honours to be commanded,
[signed] John Martyn, Mayor
John Bonnd James Bagg Robert Rawlyn Robert Trelawny Thomas Fownes

Plymouth this 24th of February 1622 [1623]

5. Certificate. Mayor and Aldermen of Barnstáple to the Privy Council, 28 February 1623.

PRO, SP14/138/109
[endorsed. To the right honourable the Lords and others of his Majesty's most honourable Privy Council.
Last day of February 1622. A certificate from *Barnestaple* about corn.]

Right honourable our bounden duties premised; according to the direction of your Lordships' letters we caused a view to be taken of all such inns and alehouses as were then within this town of *Barnestaple* and finding them to amount to an unnecessary number, we forthwith suppressed the excess, especially such as of their own authority without warrant of law presumed to brew or tipple and further we dealt with them according to the statute in that behalf made and provided. We have also taken order that no malt shall be made of barley within this town (for that God be praised) there is convenient store of oats to make malt of to serve the town and country hereabout. Moreover we have carefully provided that no man within this town shall engross any manner of grain but that the same shall be sold in the open market and not in private men's houses. Touching the rest of the Articles contained in his Majesty's Book of Orders we do and shall apply ourselves (the best we can) to see the same to be daily put in execution, howbeit we further advertise your Lordships that (notwithstanding all our care and endeavours) the price of all sorts of grain doth daily increase. And that this town and the country here about doth daily grow more and more into poverty which we pray the Lord to redress at his good will and pleasure. And so we humbly rest by your Lordships to be commanded, [signed] John Pearde, Mayor
Richard Beaple, Alderman Penticost Doddridge, Alderman

Barnestaple this last of February 1622 [1623]

6. Letter. High Sheriff of Devon to the Privy Council, received 5 April 1623.

PRO, SP14/142/37
[endorsed. To the right honourable the Lords and others of his Majesty's most honourable Privy Council.
5 April 1623.
letter from the high Sheriff of Devon concerning the provision of corn.]

May it please your Lordships to be advertised,
That whereas I have received a proclamation with Orders of directions appointed by his Majesty for the preventing and remedying of the dearth of corn and other grain in this county. The Justices of Peace within this county have

assembled themselves together according to his Majesty's directions and have called before them the high constables, petty constables and other honest persons within their several divisions to view the corn and to see the execution of these Orders. And ['that' crossed through] that the said Justices have certified unto me being Sheriff of the county of Devon their proceedings according to his Majesty's instructions. All which certificates I return up unto your Lordships as by the Book of Orders I am commanded. So recommending my service unto your Lordships I humbly take my leave and rest, your Lordships ready to be commanded,
[signed] Edmund Fortescue, Sheriff

7. Certificate. Justices of part of Wonford and moiety of Exminster hundreds to the High Sheriff of Devon, 7 February 1623.

PRO, SP14/142/37(i)
[endorsed. To the right worthy our very loving friend Edmund Fortsecue esq. high sheriff of the county of Devon.
April 1623 certificate from Exeter concerning provision of corn.]

Mr Sheriff,
According to Orders and directions from his Majesty we together with Sir Amyas Bampfeilde (who upon some special occasion is now absent) have met together and have according to his Majesty's said Orders and directions called before us the high constables of the East division of Wonford hundred and of the moitie of *Exmister* hundred together with the petty constables of every several parish within this the said divisions. And two or three of the substantial inhabitants of every of the parishes within the said divisions and have given them in charge according to the said directions. And have this present day received their Inquiry and presentments. And accordingly have taken order for the bringing into the market of Exeter, being the next market to the said divisions, so much corn weekly of all several grains until harvest next, as may be spared according to the proportion of the said presentments. And we find the prices of the several grains hereafter mentioned to be in the said market at this time, *Viz* the bushel of wheat, rye, barley, beans, peas and oats, being ten gallons or thereabouts, of wheat 7s per bushel, rye 5s 6d per bushel, barley 4s per bushel, beans 3s 8d per bushel, peas 5s ['4s 4d' crossed through] per bushel and oats 22d per bushel. And we have likewise suppressed within the said divisions all such malsters as we have thought fit. And as for badgers, regraters and corn carriers we find not any as yet but shall be careful to have an eye over them and to suppress them as occasion shall be offered and so we rest, your loving friends,
William Cary Richard Waltham Bartholomew Berrye
From the castle of *Exon* this 7th of February 1622 [1623]

8. Certificate. Justices of Crediton, West Budleigh and part of Wonford hundreds to the High Sheriff of Devon, 15 February 1623.

PRO, SP14/142/37(ii)
[endorsed. To the right worthy the high Sheriff of the county of Devon.]

Mr Sheriff,
We his Majesty's Justices of Peace dwelling within the hundreds of Crediton, West Budleigh and *Wondford* West in this county of Devon being a sub-division allotted to the care of the Justices dwelling within the same at our late general meeting for that behalf do in obedience to his Majesty's late Proclamation and Orders thereby enjoined make certificate that we the said Justices did upon the 16th day of January last past direct our precepts unto the high constables of the said hundreds to cause the under constables and other honest and substantial inhabitants within the said hundreds to the number of twelve from each hundred, to appear before us the Thursday following with instruction unto the said high constables as by the said Orders we are directed who appeared accordingly before us saving the parishes of St Thomas and Alphington within the said hundred of *Wonndford* West to whom we did declare and give charge according to the said Orders who upon Thursday then following delivered us their presentments. Whereof we having taken due consideration did forthwith give order accordingly for the weekly bringing into the market of such quantities of corn and other grain as we conceived proportionable to every man's store thereof according to our instructions mentioned in the said Orders. The market of Crediton within our said subdivision is yet plentifully furnished with corn and other grain at reasonable prices *viz* wheat 7s 8d, rye 5s 4d, barley 4s, barley malt 4s 4d, peas 5s and beans 4s. Our measure here is ten gallons. We have suppressed malsters and restrained strangers according to the said Orders and have been every market day personally present in the said market whereby the poor people have been provided of corn by our persuasion somewhat under the price of the market to their reasonable contentments and have and will pursue the rest of the said Orders with our best endeavours. There is also one other little market within the town or village of Chagford within our said subdivision within which Sir John Whiddon, one other justice dwelleth, to whose care for that the same is remote from us. We have hitherto left the said market whereof because we have not as yet heard from the said Sir John Whiddon. We cannot now make any certain certificate concerning which we have and will again write unto the said Sir John Whiddon or otherwise will ourselves take care thereof. Given under our hands at Crediton this 15th of February 1622 [1623].
[signed] John Northcot   Richard Reynell   John Davie   Edward Cotton

9. Certificate. Justices of Haytor, Teignbridge, and parts of Stanborough, Exminster and Wonford hundreds to the High Sheriff of Devon, 22 February 1623.

PRO, SP14/142/32(iii)
[endorsed. To the right worthy our assured good friend Edmund Fortescue esq.
high Sheriff of this county of Devon at *Walapitt* these.
April 1623. Certificates from the Justices of the Peace in the County of Devon
concerning provision of corn.]

Mr Sheriff,
We whose names are subscribed dwelling within this division whereunto the hundreds of Haytor, *Tenbridge* and three parishes of the hundred of Stanborough and nine parishes of the hundred of Exminster and five parishes of Wonford South have been anciently allotted and having met and conferred together ourselves about the execution of his Majesty's proclamations and Orders lately published for the preventing and remedying the dearth of grain and suppressing the multitude of those which converteth barley into malt and other things contained in the same directions do hereby advertise you as we are required to do that we have not only in person attended the markets within the same division every market day and examined all weights & measures and assizes of bread and drink and prices of all sorts of corn and grain and otherwise do endeavour to have the said markets served and supplied with all sorts of victuals at reasonable rates and punished the faults of such as we found to be bold & willfull offenders. But also we have called together at sundry meetings the high constables and petty constables and some other persons such as we['are' crossed through] esteemed to be discreet and fit for this service of every parish within this division and have given them in charge particularly in writing according as we are enjoined by the same orders and have received back again from them their several presentments under their hands upon consideration whereof (though not so thoroughly as we intend to do) we conceive and for the present have thought fit that the best wheat whereof the measures generally used in these parts is twelve gallons the bushels do not exceed eight shillings and the best rye six shillings and the best barley five shillings and the best oats whereof the measure is greater by a peck in every bushel not above three shillings four pence the bushel which price in respect of the multitude of people and scarcity of these sorts of corn doth seem to us to be reasonable and we are in good hope it will be accordingly performed and the sooner by reforming the engrosssers and regraters and restraining the excess of bakers and maulsters whereof upon our further meetings you shall understand the success. And thus with the remembrance of our best loves we rest yours to be disposed.
[signed] Edward Seymour Edward Giles Thomas Clyfford Thomas Forde

Ashburton the 22th of February 1622 [1623]
Received the 27th of February

10. Certificate. Justices of Lifton, Tavistock and Roborough hundreds to the High Sheriff of Devon, 27 February 1623.

PRO, SP14/142/32(iv)

To the Sheriff of the county of Devon
Mr Sheriff,
According to the King Majesty's direction for supplying of the country with corn & victuals we whose names are subscribed did cause all the constables & petty constables within the hundreds of *Lyfton*, Tavistock & *Rooborow* and other substantial inhabitants of every parish within the said hundreds to the number of 36 persons in all for every hundred to appear before us at Tavistock the 24th of January last & then & there did give them in charge to make inquiry of all the particulars mentioned in the printed Book sent unto us from his Majesty for direction in that behalf and withal gave them directions for dividing themselves into several companies with our best advice concerning such other circumstances as we concieved to be fit for the better expediency of that service according to his Majesty's gracious intention. And gave them until the 7th of this instant February to attend us again at the said place with their presentments which accordingly was done for every of the said parishes by which we find that within the 3 hundreds there ['was' crossed through] is some corn of all sorts in the barns, mowhays, granaries & custody of some few several persons which might spare the same to supply the markets whereupon we called all the said persons before us at a third meeting the 14th of this instant February & have according to his Majesty's direction enjoined every of them to bring into their usual markets every market day a proportionable quantity of such corn and grain as by the said presentments we find that every of them respectively may conveniently spare & there to sell the same in such sort as by the said Book is appointed. And we find that the price of wheat is at the rate of 11s the bushel of this country, [our] measure being double Winchester measure, and rye at 9s the bushel & barley at 7s the bushel. And oats at 3s[damaged] the bushel. And we have visited the markets within the said hundreds and used our best means by persuasion & otherwise to avoid the enhancing of price of corn according to his Majesty's pleasure in that behalf signified. And do not find any badgers, broggers, or regraters of corn in the said markets. And hereof we certify according to his Majesty's direction given under our hands the 27th day of February in the twentieth year of his Majesty's reign of England, France & Ireland & of Scotland the sixth and fiftieth [sic] 1622 [1623].
[signed] Thomas Wyse   Samuel Rolle   Francis Glanvill   Arthur Tremayne Alexander Maynard

11. Certificate. Justices of Coleridge and part of Stanborough hundreds to the High Sheriff of Devon, n.d.[1]

PRO, SP14/142/32(v)

Sir,
We gave commandment by our precepts to the head constables of the two hundreds of *Colrudge* and *Staboroughe* to cause the petty constables and one other substantial inhabitant of every of the several parishes within the said two hundreds to appear before us to the end that view might be taken by them of the corn within their said several parishes according to his Majesty's proclamation and directions to us in that behalf given upon which precepts the constables and one inhabitant of every of the said several parishes excepting the parish of *Hole* [Holne], *Deane* [Dean] Prior & Buckfastleigh did appear before us to whom we gave charge to take view of the corn within their said parishes and to make certificate thereof to us according to his Highness' proclamation and directions so given who have made certificate to us of their doings therein which we have sent to you by this ['bearer' crossed through] messenger according to the directions aforesaid ['but' crossed through] but none of the petty constables of the said parishes of *Hole, Deane* Prior or *Buckfasteleighe* nor any other of the inhabitants of the said parishes did appear before us neither have made to us any certificate of any view taken by them of whose neglect we have thought good also to certify you. And these & your loving friends,
[signed] William Bastard Nicholas Gilbert

To the right worshipful Edmund Fortescue esq. high Sheriff of the county of Devonshire give these.

12. Report of West Alvington parish, n.d.

PRO, SP14/144/32(v)

Westalvington	Persons	Wheat	Barley	Oats
William Bastard, esq.	22	30		
Nicolas Gilbert, esq.	36	80	120	40
Thomas Gilbert, esq.	12	20	10	40
John Cotwill, gent.	14		10	40
John Phillips	16	10	20	80
Robert Perrett	13	20	30	20
John Stevens	10	20	30	100
Richard Burdwood	14	30	40	40
William Ward	16	30	30	

West Alvington cont'd

Westalvington	Persons	Wheat	Barley	Oats
Robert Bastard	8	30	30	
James Burdwood	7	20		
John Squere	9	20		
Water Browne	8	60	20	40
John Perse		30	10	10
Elizabeth Heed	10		20	
Archilles Crispine	8		10	
James Lome sen.	5	5	60	
Thomas Cornishe	9	10		
James Lome jun.	5	20	30	50
John Pynhay	11	15	20	
Peter ['Ch' crossed through]				
Cristoin	4	30	60	
William Harradon	8	10		20
John Bomkerk	6	12		10
Samson Cotten	3	4		

Total sum in wheat 500. 4, in barley 500. 50, in oats 400. 80. 10.

13. Report of East Allington parish, n.d.

PRO. SP14/144/32(vi)

Estallyngton

The names of those within the said parish that have corn to sell & how much every one can spare of each grain.

Mr John Fortescue is 34 persons, he can spare ten bushels of barley.
Mr Moore is ten persons, he can spare threescore bushels of wheat.
Richard Roupe of *Nutecombe* [Nutcombe] he is 15 persons, he can spare 20 bushels of barley & 20 of oats.
Richard Roupe of *Cutrey* [Cuttery], is 12 persons, he can spare 6 bushels of wheat & 20 of oats.
John Dyer is 8 persons he can spare, 6 bushels of wheat.
John Yebbacomb is ten persons, he can spare 10 bushels of wheat, 10 of barley & 40 of oats.
Edmund Hyngeston is 5 persons, he can spare 6 bushels of wheat, ten bushels of barley.
Bennet Scoble is 7 persons, he can spare ten bushels of oats.
Nicholas Downynge is 7 persons, he can spare 6 bushels of wheat, 20 bushels of barley.

Humphrey Head is two persons, he can spare 20 bushels of barley & ten bushels of oats.

Nicholas Ford is 4 persons, he can spare 8 bushels of wheat, thirty bushels of barley & thirty bushels of oats.

William Cole is 7 persons, he can spare 4 bushels of wheat & ten bushels of barley.

William Hengeston is 6, persons he can spare twenty bushels of oats.

Edward Wakeham is 4 persons, he can spare 6 bushels of wheat.

John Toser is 6 persons, he can spare thirty bushels of oats.

John Laverr he can spare thirty bushels of oats.

John Scoble is 8 persons & can spare 15 bushels of wheat.

Anne Tucker is two persons & can spare 8 bushels of wheat & 6 of barley.

Sum total - 135 bushels of wheat
Sum total of barley - 132
Sum total of oats - 210   477

14. Report of Harberton parish, n.d.

PRO, SP14/144/32(vii)

Harberton	Wheat	Barley	Oats	till barley	till oats	people	spare wheat	spare barley	oats
William Wotten, esq.	80	160	140	16	20	35	spends in his house weekly 14 bushels		
Thomas Risdon, esq.	80	140	120	15	24	21	60	60	0
Mr Guine, merchant	60	250	120	20	12	16	40	150	30
Mr Martain, merchant	30	20	60	5	14	00	30	00	00
William Huxham, gent.	40	100	180	10	16	15	20	40	100
Nicholas Tippett, gent.	25	120	80	10	12	15	00	40	00
Edward Berry	10	80	80	11	13	12	00	40	40
Thomas Heyle	80	40	50	12	20	12	40	00	00
				more sold not yet delivered of wheat 27					
John Triste	10	40	40	5	4	11	00	20	20
Edward Elliott *of* Berry Pomeroy	00	90	32	8	8	00	00	70	12
John Locke	20	50	70	4	5	12	10 with malt	20	50
William Norris *of* Totnes	30	90	60	8	7	[blank]	15	30	20
Zachary Huxham	20	50	80	10	20	12	20	00	30
Marian and Peter Knowling	18	40	30	6	7	9	6	6	00
Richard Hodge	20	34	40	5	7	10	10	00	00
Mr Evory of Totnes	00	16	00	00	00	00	00	16	00
Lawrence Deyman	12	24	50	8	7	11	00	00	20

Harberton cont'd

Nicholas Evelinge	10	50	30	6	3	10	00	10	10
Thomas Tambles	20	00	00	00	00	40	10	00	00
Edward Shorte	15	45	00	9	00	5	10	00	00
The widow Berrye's tenement	00	10	20	00	00	00	00	10	20

Raters: Richard Hodge Lawrence Deyman constables & John Franckline

Sum total	580	1439	1292	168	199	[blank]	298	514	382
								of peas	10

Sum total of the corn in our parish to be spared is - 1204 bushels

15. Report of Dodbrooke parish, n.d.

PRO, SP14/144/32(viii)
[endorsed. Dodbrooke]

Dodbrooke
A note of such corn and grain as are in the barns or mowhays in Dodbrooke aforesaid.

James Weamouth hath ten persons in his house and hath of wheat 100 bushels whereof he hath sold 45 bushels which are not as yet delivered.
of barley 140 bushels and tilleth this year 30 acres of barley, of oats 80 bushels and tilleth this year 20 acres of oats.
of peas four bushels.
George Brockadon hath six persons in his house and hath of barley 25 bushels and tilleth this year 4 ['bush' crossed through] acres of barley.
of oats 25 bushels and tilleth this year 4 acres of oats.
of peas 3 bushels.
Alexander Wollcott of *Kingesbridg*['e mchte' crossed through] merchant hath of barley 120 bushels.
William Horwill of *Kingesbridge* hath of barley 20 bushels.
Robert Mudge hath six persons in his house & hath of barley 50 bushels & tilleth none.
John Luscombe hath four persons in his house & hath of barley 20 bushels and tilleth five acres of barley.
Philip Locke hath eight persons in his house and tilleth two acres & hath of barley 30 bushels.
John Michell, miller, and hath ten persons in his house and hath of barley 60 bushels & tilleth none.

Sum of the bushels - 677.

16. Report of Churchstow parish, n.d.

PRO, SP14/144/32(lx)

Churstow

Arthur Harris esq. to sell of wheat - 40 bushels
of oats and barley none - [' to sow ' crossed through] to sell
of barley and oats ['to sow' inserted] - 40 acres
of people to house - 16
John Ridere to sell of wheat - 40 bushels
of barley 40 bushels, of oats - 40 bushels
to sow of barley & oats - 20 acres
of people to house - 24
Richard Tirrie to sell of wheat -10 bushels
of barley 12 bushels, of oats - 12 bushels
of people to house - 7
to sow of oats and barley - 10 acres
William Putt to sell of barley - 10 bushels
and of oats 10 bushels, of wheat none
to sow of barley and oats - 26 acres
of people to house - 10
Edward Finch to sell of oats - 6 bushels
of wheat & barley none to sow
of barley & oats - 6 acres
of people to house - 12
['Nichol' crossed through]
Nicholas Knowlinge to sell of wheat - 8 bushels
of barley 15 bushels, of oats none
to sow of barley and oats - 6 acres
of people to house - 6
John Tallman to sell of wheat - 8 bushels
of oats 4 bushels, of barley none
to sow of oats & barley - 12 acres
of people to house - 8
John Head to sell of barley - 6 bushels
of wheat and oats none
to sow of barley and oats - 15 acres
of people to house - 9
Andrew Bardenes to sell of oats - 20 bushels
Matthew Castellman to sell of wheat 12 bushels
Pascow Warde to sell of wheat - 30 bushels
of barley - 40 bushels
of oats - 10 bushels
to sow of barley and oats - 10 acres   *Total sum* 343 [bushels]

17. Report of Woodleigh parish, n.d.

PRO, SP14/144/32(x)

Woodley

Francis Fortescue esq. hath 23 people to house, wheat 40 bushels, barley 100 bushels, ground to sow for barley 14 acres, 60 bushels of *wootts*, ground to sow for *wotts* 22 acres.

Elizabeth Hurrell widow, 22 people to house, of wheat 40 bushels, of barley 100 bushels, ground to sow for barley 10 acres, of *wotts* 80 bushels, ground to sow for *wotts* 25 acres.

Elizabeth Parnell widow 11 people to house, of wheat 50 bushels of barley 120 bushels, ground to sow six barley 6 acres, of *wotts* 50 bushels, ground to sow for *wotts* 18 acres.

Tristram Blunte 13 people to house, wheat none; of barley of barley [sic] 80 bushels, ground to sow for barley 22 acres, of *wotts* 100 bushels; ground to sow for *wotts* 20 acres.

John Hurrell hath 10 people to house, of wheat 20 bushels, of barley 60 bushels, ground to sow for barley 10 acres, of *wotts* 80 bushels, ground to sow for *wotts* 18 acres.

Arthur Hurrell 12 people to house; of wheat 14 bushels, of barley 50 bushels, ground to sow for barley 7 acres, of *wotts* 30 bushels, ground to sow for *wotts* 14 acres.

John Bastard 6 people to house, wheat none; barley 40 bushels, ground to sow none, *wotts* none.

Anthony Gowde 4 people to house, of wheat none, barley none, of *wotts* 30 bushels, ground to sow for *wotts* ['no' crossed through] 2 acres.

Sum total of wheat	164 bushels	[signed] William Hurrell
Sum total of barley	550 bushels	Roger Adam Constables
Sum total of *wotts*	430 bushels	Robert Yeabsley Rater

18. Report of East Portlemouth parish, n.d.

PRO, SP14/144/32(xi)

Eastportlemouth

A note how many persons every man hath in his house, how many acres of corn he till and what corn every man hath.

Mr John Neele hath in his house fourteen persons he tilleth three score acres of barley & oats and hath twenty bushels of wheat, one hundred of barley &

one hundred and fifty of oats.

Roger Crispine hath in his house eight persons he tilleth twenty acres of barley & oats & hath four bushels of wheat, fifty of barley & threescore of oats.

Robert Abraim hath in his house ten persons, he tilleth thirty acres of barley & oats & hath twenty bushels of wheat, four score of barley & threescore of oats.

Robert Bevill hath in his house eight persons, he tilleth 12 acres of barley & oats & hath thirty bushels of wheat ['whe' crossed through], four of barley and fifty of oats.

Johan Lamball hath in her house eight persons, she tilleth five acres of barley & oats & hath eight bushels of wheat, forty of barley and ten of oats.

Johan Stone hath in her house six persons, she tilleth seven acres of barley & oats & hath eight bushels of wheat, thirty of barley and twenty of oats.

Walter Cornish hath in his house six persons, he tilleth six acres of barley & oats & hath ten bushels of wheat, thirty of barley & six of oats.

Susan Cornish hath in her house seven persons, she tilleth four acres of barley & oats & hath twenty bushels of barley.

Matthew Cornish hath in his house six persons, he tilleth six acres of barley & oats & hath fifteen bushels of wheat and threescore of barley.

Richard Vinson hath in his house three persons, he tilleth four acres of barley & oats, & hath ten bushels of wheat & twenty of barley.

Peter Jillerd hath in his house eight persons, he tilleth five acres of barley & oats and hath twenty bushels of wheat, forty of barley & twenty of oats.

19. Report of Sherford parish, n.d.

PRO, SP14/144/32(xii)

Shearford

A note of corn how much every man can spare within our parish viewed by John Teallor, Constable, and Richard Browne, Rator, their sale allowed.

Mr George Reynell esq. he can spare 10 bushels of wheat
Mr Nicholas Reynell, his seed allowed, he can spare 40 bushels of wheat, 60 bushels of barley and 20 bushels of oats
Mr John Edwardes he can spare 80 bushels of barley and 40 bushels of oats.
Mr Arthur Wackham he can spare 60 bushels of barley and 20 bushels of oats
Nichlas Lucke he can spare 80 bushels of barley
Richard Browne he can spare 10 bushels of barley
Richard Coorworthie he can spare 20 bushels of barley
Richard Weekes he can spare 12 bushels of wheat

Sum total 62 bushels of wheat, 310 bushels of barley and 80 bushels of oats.

Sherford cont'd
Mr George Reynell esq. hath persons 32
Mr Nicholas Reynell hath persons 20
Mr John Edwards hath persons 12
Mr Arthur Wackham hath persons 11
Mr Nicholas Lucke hath persons 4
Richard Browne hath persons 8
Richard Coorworthie hath persons 5
Richard Weeks hath persons 6

20. Report of Moreleigh parish, n.d.

PRO, SP14/144/32(xiii)
[endorsed. *Moreley.*]

Moreley

A note of the names of such as can spare and sell corn there, the numbers of bushels of corn and grain in barns threshed and unthreshed, of persons in their houses and acres they till to barley and oatland. *Vizt:*

First Philip Slure esq. hath in his house - 20 persons
Item he hath of wheat - 30 bushels
Item he hath of barley - 40
Item he hath of oats - 240
Item he ['hath of' crossed through] tilleth to barley land - 20 acres
Item he tilleth to oatland - 35 acres
Item he can spare & sell only - 100 bushels of oats

Item William Luscombe hath in his house - 11 persons
Item he hath of wheat - 7 bushels
Item he hath of barley - ['50' crossed through] 50
Item he hath of oats - 140
Item he tills of barley land - 8 acres
Item he tills of oatland - 18 acres
Item he can sell - 60 bushels of oats

Item John Oldreive hath in his house - 12 persons
Item he hath of wheat - 10 bushels
Item he hath of barley - 20
Item he hath of oats - 100
Item he tilles of barley land - 6 acres
Item he tilles of oatland - 20 acres

Item he can spare only of oats - 20 bushels of oats

Item Elizabeth Hurrell, widow, hath in her house - 12 persons
Item she hath of wheat - 70 bushels
Item she hath of barley - 70
Item she hath of oats - 160
Item she tills barley land - 15 acres
Item she tills of oatland - 18 acres
Item she can spare of wheat - 50 bushels
Item she can spare of oats - 80

Item John Hurrell hath in his house - 9 persons
Item he hath of wheat - 10 bushels
Item he hath of barley - 30
Item he hath of oats - 30
Item he tills of barley land - 4 acres
Item he tills of oatland - 7 acres
Item he can spare & sell of wheat - 3 bushels
Item he can spare & sell of oats - 12

Item David Oldreive hath in his house - 10 persons
Item he hath of wheat - none
Item he hath of barley - 20 bushels
Item he hath of oats - 30
Item he tills of barley land - 4 acres
Item he tills of oatland - 12 acres
Item he hath a mill the increase whereof he seils to poor people by pecks & half
pecks except such as he spends in his house

Item Tristram Blunte of *Woodley* [Woodleigh] hath in a barn in
Grimsoonsleighe [Grimpstonleigh] in a barn & in a mowhay being within our
parish of wheat - 120 bushels

The whole number of bushels of the parishioners - 1057
Tristram Blunt's - 120
In all 1177

To spare of the parishioners - 325
of Blunt's - 120
In all - 445

[signed]William Luscomb   Constable
John Tainlyng

21. Report of South Milton parish, n.d.

PRO, SP14/144/32(xiv)

South Milton

Christopher Lapthorne hath 20 bushels of wheat & 4 bushels of peas to sell; 18 persons to house.
William Gilberde hath 10 bushels of wheat & 10 bushels of oats to sell; 12 persons to house.
Robert Strode hath 6 bushels of wheat & 6 bushels of barley to sell; 7 persons to house.
Hugh Michell hath 20 bushels of wheat to sell; 12 persons to house.
Walter Avent hath 6 bushels of wheat to sell; 8 persons to house.
Robert Seare hath 30 bushels of wheat to sell; 10 persons to house.
William Hingeston hath 20 bushels of wheat to sell; 7 persons to house.
John Luckcrafte hath 4 bushels of wheat to sell; 5 persons to house.
Alexander Michell hath 16 bushels of wheat; 12 bushels of barley & 20 bushels of oats to sell.
Walter Striche hath 20 bushels of barley to sell; 7 persons to house.
Andrew Harwarde hath 12 bushels of wheat to sell; 6 persons to house.
Richard Harwarde hath 4 bushels of wheat, 10 bushels of barley & 10 bushels of oats to sell; 5 persons to house.

7 score & 8 bushels of wheat
4 bushels of peas
48 bushels of barley
40 bushels of oats   The whole sum is 12 score bushels

22. Report of Kingsbridge borough, n.d.

PRO, SP14/144/32(xv)

Kingsbrige

John Lappr - 6 persons - 20 bushels of barley - 20 bushels of ['whea' crossed through] oats.
Margaret Yeabbe - 7 persons - 10 bushels of wheat - 40 of barley - 10 of oats.
Mr Richard Ryche of *Blacke Autton* [Blackawton] of wheat, barley & oats - 30 bushels.

23. Report of Loddiswell parish, n.d.

PRO, SP14/144/32(xvi)

Loddeswill

A note what people every person here underwritten hath in his house, how many ac[?'res of' torn] wheat, barley and oats he soweth & how many bushels of the like he can spare to the in[torn] this year particularly here ensueth.

	People in house	acres of barley	acres of oats	acres of wheat	bushels of wheat	bushels of barley	b[ushels] of [oats]
Mr Clement Elis	hath 21	hath sown 13	will sow 13	13	can spare 10	0	0
Mr John Grinte	hath 20	hath sown 6	will sow 20	20	can spare 20	20	10
Simon Philips and his two sons	have 26	hath sown 18	will sow 30	15	can spare 40	40	
John Lovecraft and his two sons	have 19	hath sown 14	will sow 6	14	can spare 10	30	
John Gill and his two sons	have 16	hath sown 10	will sow 12	18	can spare 0	10	20
Philip Phillips	hath 13	hath sown 6	will sow 8	5	can spare 5	10	5
Thomas King	hath 12	hath sown 4	will sow 8	5	can spare 10	0	20
John Swadle	hath 8	hath sown 6	will sow 6	5	can spare 0	0	1
Philip Avent	hath 8	hath sown 6	will sow 6	8	can spare 0	0	
Cicelie Phillipps	hath 8	hath sown 4	will sow 8	0	can spare 5	5	
WilliamPhillipps	hath 12	hath sown 1½	will sow 4	2	can spare 0	10	
Thomas Phillipps the younger	hath 0	hath sown 0	will sow 0	1½	can spare 0	10	
					100	135	1[torn]

Stephen Oldreiffe
Philip Avent   constables   *total sum* 350

24. Report of North Huish parish, n.d.

PRO, SP14/144/32(xvii)

North *Huishe*

A note of all men's names which are to spare corn within our parish as near as we can discern to our knowledge as followeth, 1622.

George Prestwoode esq. wheat & rye 100 bushels, barley two hundred bushels, oats 100 bushels & he doth sow to oats twenty-four acres & unto barley twenty five acres, persons 36.
Anthony Harvie barley 60 bushels, oats 60 bushels & he doth sow to oats 12 acres & to barley 12 acres, persons 17.

North Huish cont'd

Peter Maddocke wheat 40 bushels, barley 60 bushels, oats fourscore bushels & he doth sow to oats 20 acres & to barley eight acres, persons twelve.

John Hine wheat 20 bushels, barley 30 bushels, oats 40 bushels & he sow to oats 7 acres & to barley 6 acres, persons nine.

John Prowse wheat 10 bushels, barley 30 bushels, oats 30 bushels and he doth sow to oats 7 acres & to barley 12 acres, persons 7.

Thomas Harvie wheat 12 bushels, barley 30, oats 30 bushels & he doth sow 6 acres to oats & to barley 4, persons 8.

Walter Soper wheat 20 bushels, barley 20, oats 100 bushels & he doth sow to oats 20 acres to barley 3 acres, persons 11.

Peter Wyate wheat 20 bushels, barley 30 bushels, oats 30 bushels & he doth sow to oats 3 acres & to barley 3 acres, persons 15.

Anne Welbrocke wheat 15 bushels, persons 6.

Roger Heard 15 bushels of wheat, persons 7.

Arthur Hurrell of *Woodelye* [Woodleigh] hath in our parish one mowhay of wheat and barley and one other of oats by estimation of wheat and barley a 100 bushels and of oats 4 score.

The full sum of corn in our parish of North *Huishe* amounteth to thirteen hundred and threescore bushels.

[signed] John Andrews Thomas Harvye Constables   Peter Wyatt

25. Report of South Huish parish, n.d.

PRO, SP14/144/32(xviii)

Southhewsh

The names of them that have corn to sell

Thomas Crispin of wheat - 5 - bushels & persons - 12
Edward Crauch of wheat - 20 - bushels & persons - 15
Heugh Edwardes of wheat - 40 - bushels & of persons - 12
John Hingston of wheat - 30 - bushels & of oats - 30 - bushels   persons 12
Issac Pearnes of wheat - 20 - bushels & of persons - 13
John Dew of wheat - 40 - bushels & of persons - 6

Sum total of wheat 200 bushels and of oats - 30 bushels

26. Report of Charleton parish, n.d.

PRO SP14/144/32(xix)

The parish of *Charelton* of corn hath to spare & their household maintained & their ground to be served of wheat 244 bushels & of barley 513 bushels & of oats 200 bushels so the whole sum of wheat, barley & oats is 967 bushels & the names of them that do spare it.

	wheat	barley	oats	and this many in their houses	of barley to sow acres	of oats to sow acres
Henry Luke	10	20	20	10	15	10
Richard Winchelsey	2	12	20	10	5	1
Joan Pearce	3	0	20	5	0	4
William Corkerey	3	0	0	4	0	0
William Taverner	5	10	0	4	7	0
Nicholas Browne	4	10	0	7	4	0
Anne Tomme	6	10	0	5	5	0
William Winchelsey	14	20	0	15	8	0
Roger Gonfilde	0	10	0	3	9	0
James Earell	0	60	0	5	8	0
Richard Winchelsey	2	5	0	7	4	0
John Tozer	5	0	0	6	0	0
James Smeith	30	60	10	4	6	4
Richard Smeith	0	6	10	7	10	5
William Wakhame	6	30	10	9	7	14
John Bastard	0	30	0	7	14	0
William Gonnfilde	0	10	10	9	4	3
Richard Stone	6	60	0	8	6	0
William Luke	30	60	30	9	4	10
William Kinge	25	10	0	0	0	0
John Helmore	4	6	0	7	3	0
William Banndell	4	10	10	11	12	10
Mary Phellippes	0	10	10	7	15	13
Mr Philip Hurrell	10	10	10	7	15	13
John Wakham	40	0	0	8	0	0
John Bevell	12	0	6	6	0	0
William Cleiffe	0	0	30	17	0	19
Edmund Warden	3	4	0	5	3	0
Thomas Fostard	0	0	0	6	10	0
John Torbe	10	0	0	8	0	0
the sum	244	513	200			

27. Report of Stokenham parish, n.d.

PRO, SP14/144/32(xx)
[endorsed. *Stokeingham.*]

Stokeingham

Mr John Hodge persons - 16
may spare of wheat bushels - 25
of barley - 30
soweth of barley acres - 10
of oats - 9

John Hyne persons - 8
may spare of wheat bushels - 40
soweth of barley acres - 3
of oats - 2

Elizabeth Hedd persons - 3
may spare of wheat bushels - 10
of barley - 20
soweth of barley acres - 5
of oats - 4

Michael Wakeham persons - 7
may spare of barley bushels - 10
soweth of barley acres - 5
of oats - 3

William Gould persons - 14
may spare of wheat - 15
of barley - 20
soweth of barley acres - 8
of oats - 7

Thomas Vinter persons - 10
may sow of wheat bushels -10
of barley - 30
of oats - 30
soweth of barley acres - 7
of oats - 6

Sylfine Hedd persons - 10
may spare of wheat bushels - 50
of barley - 20
of oats - 20
soweth of barley acres - 10
of oats - 8

Nicholas Perrott persons - 5
may spare of wheat bushels - 50
of barley - 40
of oats - 50
soweth of barley acres - 10
of oats - 7

Peter Wakeham persons - 11
may spare of wheat bushels - 30
soweth of barley acres - 9
of oats - 10

Edward Prall persons - 9
may spare of wheat bushels - 10
soweth of barley acres - 4

Richard Luscomb persons - 14
May spare of wheat bushels - 30
of ['oats' crossed through] barley
bushels - 40
Soweth of barley acres - 12
of oats - 7

William Chubb persons - 13
may spare of wheat bushels - 6
of barley - 80
soweth of barley acres - 4

Nicholas Hawkings persons - 8
may spare of wheat bushels - 6
soweth of barley acres - 6
of oats acres - 5

Philip Peradon persons - 8
may spare of wheat bushels - 20
of oats bushels - 6
soweth of barley acres - 7
of oats - 4

Michael Werren persons - 9
may spare of bushels - 30
soweth of barley acres - 14
of oats acres - 30

Michael Phillip persons - 5
may spare of oats bushels - 10
soweth of barley acres - 4
of oats acres - 3

Nicholas Horswyll
John Horswill persons - 8
bought in the ground
 of barley acres - 10
may spare of barley bushels - 40

Richard Milton persons - 8
may spare of wheat bushels - 10
of barley - 20
of oats - 12
soweth of barley acres - 9
of oats acres - 8

Wilmote Cole persons - 4
may spare of barley bushels - 4
of oats - 10
soweth of barley acres - 5
of oats - 4

Robert Knight persons - 11
may spare of wheat bushels - 20
of barley - 20
of oats bushels - 20
soweth of barley acres - 8
of oats - 6

Allen Werren persons - 12
may spare of wheat - 10
of barley - 10
soweth of barley acres - 9
of oats - 5

Amos Derrie persons - 9
may spare of wheat bushels - 10
soweth of barley acres - 12
of oats acres - 10

Robert Edwards persons - 8
may spare of barley - 20
of oats - 20
soweth of barley acres - 8
of oats - 2

Total Sum 963

28. Report of Thurlestone parish, n.d.

PRO, SP14/144/32(xxi)

Thurleston

The names of them that did view the corn John Sheppard, William Tabbe and John Randell.
The names of them have the corn are here under written.

First
Mr Luscum hath of wheat 80 bushels, of barley 80 bushels.
Item he doth sow six acres of barley & he hath in his house 9 persons.
Mr Stephens he hath of wheat 100 bushels, of barley 300 bushels and of oats 60 bushels and he hath in his house 27 persons. Item he doth sow 40 acres of barley and twenty acres of oats.
Philip Cornishe of wheat 60 bushels and of barley 100 bushels & of oats 50 bushels and he doth sow to barley 20 acres and to oats 12 acres and he hath in his house 14 persons.
John Sheppard hath of barley 100 bushels and of oats 40 bushels and he doth sow to barley 17 acres and to oats 10 acres and he hath in his house 9 persons.
Johan Liddeson, widow, ['did' crossed through] hath of barley 20 bushels and she doth sow none and she hath in her house five persons.
Elizabeth Phillipes, widow, she hath of wheat 15 bushels, of ['oats' crossed through] barley 60 bushels and of oats 30 bushels and she hath in her house 7 persons and she doth sow to barley 7 7 [sic] acres and to oats 6 acres.
John Phillipes hath of wheat 4 bushels, of barley 50 bushels, of oats 30 and he doth sow to barley 10 acres and to oats 6 acres and he hath in his house 12 persons.
Nicholas Pearce hath of wheat 12 bushels and of barley 50 bushels and of oats none and he doth sow to barley 6 acres and he hath in his house five persons.
Johan Cornishe, widow, she hath of wheat 30 bushels and of barley 40 bushels and of oats 40 bushels and she doth sow to barley 9 acres and to oats 7 acres and she hath in her house 8 persons.
Robert Cornishe he hath of wheat 30 bushels and of barley 30 bushels and of oats 20 bushels and he doth sow to barley 6 acres and to oats 6 acres and he hath in his house 9 persons.
John Randell he hath of barley 60 bushels and of oats 16 bushels and he doth sow of barley 8 acres and of oats 4 acres and he hath in his house 9 persons.
Andrew Pildiche he hath of barley 50 bushels and of oats 20 bushels.
Item he doth sow to barley 8 acres and to oats 6 acres & he hath in his house 7 persons.
David Yolman he hath of barley 30, of oats 10 bushels and he doth sow to barley five acres and to oats 2 acres & in his house [damaged]

Nicholas Barry he hath of wheat 20 bushels and of barley 10 bushels and he [damaged] sow to barley 4 acres and to oats 3 acres & he hath in his house 6 persons.

Andrew Crispine he hath of barley 20 bushels & no oats and he doth sow to barley 2 acres and he hath in his house 6 persons.

Richard Drewe he hath of wheat 40 bushels and of barley 40 bushels and he hath in his house 4 persons.

Andrew Rogers jun. he hath of barley 20 bushels and of oats 20 bushels and he doth sow to barley 2 acres and to oats 2 acres and he hath in his house 10 persons.

Mr Dotinge he hath of wheat 40 bushels, of oats 20 bushels and no barley and he doth sow to barley 8 acres and his oats is all sown and he hath in his house 14 persons.

Wilmote Langman, widow, she hath of barley 20 bushels, of oats 10 bushels and she doth sow of barley 4 acres and of oats 2 acres and she hath in her house 7 persons.

Thomas Yolman he hath of barley 60 bushels, of oats 20 bushels and he doth sow of barley 7 acres and of oats 2 acres and he hath in his house 8 persons.

Andrew Rogers sen. he hath of barley 100 bushels, of oats 60 bushels and he doth sow to barley 17 acres and to oats 12 acres & he hath in his house 15 persons.

Robert Tuckam he hath of barley 40 bushels, of oats 10 bushels and he doth sow to barley 5 acres and to oats 3 acres and he hath in his house 5 persons.

John Langman he hath of barley 20 bushels, of oats 10 bushels and he doth sow to barley 3 acres and to oats 2 acres and he hath in his house 8 persons.

Robert Liddeson he hath of barley 20 bushels, of oats 10 bushels and he doth sow to barley 2 acres and to oats 2 acres and he hath in his house 6 persons.

William Tabbe he hath of barley 40 bushels and of oats 10 bushels and he doth sow of barely 4 acres and of oats 2 acres and he hath in his house 9 persons.

John Drew he hath of barley 30 bushels and no oats and he doth sow ['of' crossed through] to barley 3 acres and he hath in his house 5 persons.

Total sum of the wheat is - 431
of barley the sum is - 1390
and of oats - 486 So the whole sum is 2037 bushels.

29. Report of Malborough parish, n.d.

PRO, SP14/144/32(xxii)

Malborough
The names of them that have corn to sell.

Philip Harris hath in his house 16 persons & he hath of wheat 250 bushels, of barley 340 bushels and doth sow to barley and oats 56 acres.

William Weimont hath in his house 16 persons and hath of wheat 120 bushels, of barley 200 bushels & of oats 200 bushels and doth sow to barley 28 acres and to oats 22 acres.

Hugh Perrot hath in his house 15 persons and hath of wheat 20 bushels, of barley 200 bushels & of oats 150 bushels and doth sow to barley & oats 30 acres.

John & Richard Adams have in their house 18 persons & have of wheat 40 bushels, of barley 100 bushels & of oats 30 bushels and they sow to barley and oats 16 acres.

John Weimont of *Lincomb* [e] hath in his house 12 persons & he hath of barley 140 bushels & of oats 60 bushels & doth sow to barley 12 acres & to oats 11 acres.

Nicholas Adams hath in his house 9 persons & he hath of wheat 30 bushels, of barley 40 40 [sic] & of oats 6 bushels & doth sow to barley 6 acres & to oats 3 acres.

Owen Weimont hath in his house 12 persons & hath of wheat 16 bushels, of barley 80 bushels & of oats 50 bushels & doth sow to barely 8 acres & to oats 4 acres.

John Adam & Robert his son have in their house 12 persons & have of wheat 50 bushels, of barley 60 bushels & of oats 20 bushels they sow to barley 6 acres & to oats 2 acres.

Thomas Adam in his house 7 persons & he hath of wheat 40 bushels, of barley 30 acres & of oats 30 bushels & doth sow to barley 4 acres & to oats 2 acres.

Edmund Adam in his house 6 persons he hath of wheat ['40' crossed through] 8 bushels, of barley 30 bushels & he doth sow to barley and oats 4 acres.

John Edwards in his house 11 persons, he hath of wheat 40 bushels, of barley 80 bushels, of oats 20 bushels, he doth sow to barley 6 acres & to oats 4 acres.

Roger Birdwood in his house 10 persons he hath of wheat 20 bushels, of barley 30 bushels & of oats 20 bushels, he doth sow of barley 6 acres of of [sic] oats 3 acres.

John Hingston in his house 15 persons he hath of wheat 40 bushels, of barley 80 bushels, of oats 60 bushels & doth sow of barley 15 acres and of oats 15 acres.

Stephen Clarke in his house 10 persons he hath of barley 40 bushels & of oats 40 bushels & doth sow of barley 6 acres & of oats 5 acres.

Henry Pollexfen in his house 8 persons, he hath of wheat 10 bushels, of barley

80 bushels, of oats 60 bushels. He doth sow of barley 22 acres [and] of oats 8 acres.

Philip Evans in his house 10 persons. He hath of wheat 8 bushels, of barley 40 bushels, of oats 12 bushels, he doth sow of barley 6 acres, of oats 4 acres.

Ambrose Roades in his house 4 persons he hath of rye 20 bushels, of wheat 8 bushels, of barley 10 bushels, of oats 20 bushels & doth sow of barley 2½ acres, of oats 8 acres.

James Nicholls in his house 10 persons, he hath of barley 50 bushels, of oats 40 bushels, he doth sow to barley 7 acres and to oats 6 acres.

Samuel Evans in his house 7 persons, he hath of wheat 10 bushels of barley 16 bushels of oats ['6 b' crossed through] 8 bushels, he doth sow of barley 4 acres & of oats 2 acres.

Andrew Luckum in his house 10 persons he hath of wheat 16 bushels, of barley 40 bushels of oats 20 bushels, he doth sow of barley 4 acres, of oats 5 acres.

Walter Peirse in his house 9 persons he hath of wheat 12 bushels, of barley 50 bushels, of oats 20 bushels, he doth [sow] of barley 3 acres, of oats 8 acres.

William Adam in his house 8 persons he hath of barley 50 bushels, of oats 30 bushels & doth sow of barley 7 acres & of oats 6 acres.

Richard Evans in his house 9 persons he hath of wheat 6 bushels, of barley 40 bushels, of oats 40 bushels, he doth sow of barley 8 acres & of oats 15 acres.

Total sum   of wheat is 736 bushels, of barley 1826 bushels
of oats 941 bushels, of rye 20 bushels

30. Report of South Brent parish, n.d.

PRO, SP14/144/32(xxiii)
[endorsed. To be delivered to Mr Gest, Mr Webber's clerk at *Kingesbridge*.]

Brent

A note of the corn that is in the custody of those whose names are here under written and how many acres of barley and oats they purpose to sow this year and the number of company every of them keep in their houses besides workmen as followeth:

First

John Prowse of Moore hath in his custody 30 bushels of wheat, 60 bushels of barley and 70 bushels of oats, 20 acres of oats and 14 acres of barley to be sown & hath in his house persons - 16.

John Stidston hath in his custody 30 bushels of wheat, 20 bushels of barley & 60 bushels of oats, 12 acres of oats & 4 acres of barley to be sown, persons sixteen in his house.

South Brent cont'd

Henry Veale hath in his custody 30 bushels of wheat & rye, 60 bushels of barley & 80 bushels of oats, 10 acres of barley & 20 of oats to be sown, persons 16 in his house.

John Luscombe hath in his custody 30 bushels of wheat, 30 bushels of barley & 60 bushels of oats. 16 acres of oats & 9 acres of barley to be sown, persons 18 in his house.

Richard Harris hath in his custody 30 bushels of of [sic] wheat, 16 bushels of barley, 100 bushels of oats, three acres of barley & 8 acres of oats to be sown, 8 persons in his house.

John Collinge hath in his custody 10 bushels of wheat, 30 bushels of barley & 40 bushels of oats, 8 acres of oats & 7 acres of barley to be sown, persons 13 in his house.

Henry Maddocke hath in his custody 12 bushels of wheat, 20 bushels of barley & 50 bushels of oats, 9 acres of oats & 3 acres of barley to be sown, persons 6 in his house.

William Luscomb hath in his custody 15 bushels of wheat, 12 bushels of barley & 25 bushels of oats, 3 acres of barley & 6 acres of oats to be sown, persons eight to his house.

William Stidston hath in his custody 6 bushels of wheat, 6 bushels of barley & 35 bushels of oats, 3 acres of barley & 8 acres of oats to be sown, doth not keep house.

John Simons hath in his custody of wheat 20 bushels, of barley 30, of oats 60 bushels and doth sow 6 acres of barley & 10 acres of oats, persons 8 in his house

Ann Hannaford, widow, hath in hi['s' crossed through]r custody 20 bushels of wheat, 40 bushels of barley & 80 bushels of oats. She doth sow 12 acres of oats & 4 acres of barley, persons 12 in her house.

Pascow Fluet hath in his house 10 bushels of wheat, 16 bushels of barley & 60 bushels of oats, he doth sow 3 acres of barley & 16 acres of oats, persons 12 in his house.

Margery Veale, widow, hath in her custody 10 bushels of wheat, 20 bushels of barley & 20 bushels of oats, she doth sow 4 acres of barley & 9 acres of oats, persons 12 in her house.

William Gill hath in his custody 20 bushels of wheat, 50 bushels of barley & 80 bushels of oats and h[torn] doth sow 19 acres of oats & 12 acres of barley, persons - 14 in his house.

Henry Ford hath in his custody - 10 bushels of wheat, 50 bushels of barley, 50 bushels of oats and he doth sow 7 acres of barley & 14 ['4' crossed through] acres of oats, persons - 9 in his house.

William Norris hath in his custody 6 bushels of wheat and rye, 20 bushels of barley and 50 bushels of oats and he hath 16 acres of oats & 4 acres of barley to be sown, persons 10 in his house.

Nicholas Harvie hath in his custody 23 bushels of wheat, 30 bushels of barley & 20 bushels of oats whereof he hath sold to Alexander Halfe of Rattery, miller,

20 bushels of wheat and 20 of barley not yet delivered and he doth sow two acres of barley & seven acres of oats, persons 6 in his house.

William Simons hath in his custody 10 bushels of wheat, 16 bushels of barley, 50 bushels of oats, he doth sow 4 acres of barley & 10 acres of oats, persons 17 in his house.

James Efford hath in his custody 16 bushels of wheat, 30 bushels of barley and 50 bushels of oats and he doth sow 7 acres of barley, 12 acres of oats, persons 10 in his house.

Philip Veale hath in his custody 7 bushels of wheat & rye, 14 bushels of barley & 50 bushels of oats, he doth sow 3 acres of barley & 11 acres of oats, persons 8 in his house.

We do find in this book of wheat - 200. 90. 9. bushels
We do find in this book of barley -500. 40. 4. bushels
We do find in this book of oats - a thousand bushels

We do find in this book acres of barley to be sown - 200. 10.
We do find acres of oats to be sown -   200. 20

We do sow in every ['acre' crossed through] acre of barley - 3 bushels
We do sow in every acre of oats - 3 bushels

William Norris & Henry Ford Constables
John Lowde & Robert Foott Viewers of the corn

31. Report of Diptford parish, n.d.

PRO, SP14/144/32(xxiv)

Dipford

A note of all men's names which are to spare corn within our parish as near as we can depose to our knowledge. As followeth:

Peter Harvey hath 30 bushels of wheat & 30 of barley and of rye 10 bushels and of oats 80 bushels.
And he doth sow to oats 18 acres and unto barley 6 acres.
And he hath 16 people in his house.
Henry Downinge hath 40 bushels of wheat and of barley 30 bushels and a hundred bushels of oats. And he doth sow twenty acres of oats and 6 ['bushels' crossed through] acres of barley and he hath ten people in his house.

Diptford cont'd

Richard Towe hath 16 bushels of wheat and four bushels of rye and 30 bushels of barley and 50 bushels of oats. And he doth sow 19 acres of oats and 4 ['bushels' crossed through] acres of barley and he hath 9 people in his house.

Richard Jackson hath 40 bushels of wheat and 30 of barley and of oats four score and he doth sow 14 acres of oats and of barley 4 acres and he doth keep eleven people in his house.

Steven Binmoure hath 15 bushels of wheat and 25 of barley and of oats 30 bushels and he doth sow 9 acres of oats and 4 acres of barley and he doth keep in his house 7 people.

George Smith hath 10 bushels of wheat and 30 bushels of barley and 30 bushels of oats and he doth sow 6 acres of oats and 3 acres of barley and he doth keep in his house 7 people.

William Lavers hath 10 bushels of wheat and 40 bushels of barley & 40 bushels of oats and 2 bushels of rye and he doth sow 13 acres of oats & 5 acres of barley and he doth keep in his house 12 people.

Nicholas Hingston hath 10 bushels of wheat and 20 bushels of barley & 30 bushels of oats and he doth sow 11 acres of oats 6 acres of barley and he doth keep in his house nine people.

Andrew Downinge hath 10 bushels of wheat & 10 of ['yh' crossed through] rye and of oats 50 and of barley 30 and he doth sow 11 acres of oats and 4 acres of barley and he doth keep in his house 7 people.

The full and whole sum of all the corn with[in] our whole parish of *Dipford* amounteth unto eight hundred fourscore and twelve bushels.

[signed] Thomas Parnell Constable
          Steven Binmoure

32. Report of Blackawton parish, n.d.

PRO, SP14/144/32(xxv)

Account of the corn within our parish of *Blackaueton.*

Mr Richard Rich hath forty bushels of wheat & twenty bushels of rye and fifty bushels of barley & twenty bushels of oats & must sow within our parish 7 acres of barley and his company 28 persons.

Edward Luscombe hath fifty bushels of wheat and one hundred bushels of barley & one hundred bushels of oats & must sow 16 acres of barley & 17 of oats & his company 18 persons.

John Brasie hath forty bushels of wheat & fifty bushels of barley and thirty bushels of oats & must sow 7 acres of barley & 5 of oats & his company 6 persons.

William Holdidge hath thirty bushels of wheat & fifty bushels of barley & thirty of oats & must sow 5 acres of barley & 6 of oats & his company 5 persons.

Nicholas Colling hath sixteen bushels of wheat and forty bushels of barley & threescore bushels of oats & must sow 5 acres of barley & 11 of oats & his company 10 persons.

John Colling hath thirty bushels of wheat & fifty bushels of barley & ten of rye & threescore bushels of oats & must sow 8 acres of barley & 13 of oats & his company 12 persons.

Lewis Tucker hath thirty bushels of wheat & 15 of rye & forty of barley & threescore of oats & must sow 6 acres of barley & 16 of oats & his company 13 persons.

William Pinhey hath thirty bushels of wheat & forty bushels of barley & forty of oats & must sow 8 acres of barley & 8 of oats & his company 9 persons.

Nicholas Hinston hath forty bushels of wheat & forty of barley & forty of oats & must sow 8 acres of barley and two of oats & his company 8 persons.

Andrew Hine hath ten bushels of wheat & fifty bushels of barley & threescore bushels of oats & must sow 7 acres of barley & 11 of oats & his company 8 persons.

Robert Pinhey hath thirty bushels of wheat & fourscore bushels of barley & one hundred of oats & must sow 13 acres of barley & 17 of oats & his company 12 persons.

Richard Peryng hath twenty bushels of wheat & fifty bushels of barley & fourscore of oats & must sow 10 acres of barley and 14 of oats and his company 12 persons.

So the total sum is one thousand, seven hundred and forty 6 bushels.

33. Report of Dartington parish, 8 February 1623.

PRO, SP14/144/32(xxvi)
Devon   Dartington

Edward Skinner, Allen Sarell & John Tonker being appointed by his Majesty's Justices for the viewing of the barns and mowhays in the parish aforesaid bringing in their presentment the 8th of February the year of our Lord God 1622 [1623].

Mr Champernowne no corn to spare keeps 40 people to house.
Mr Roger Marten 100 bushels of barley to ['sell' crossed through] spare & doth till 12 acres, keeps no house.
Mr Lawrence Adems 10 bushels of wheat & 12 of barley to sell tills 18 acres is - 16 people to house.

Dartington cont'd

Allen Sarell 6 bushels of wheat & 12 of barley is 20 people to house, tills 12 acres.

John Wrefford of wheat & rye 12 bushels, 10 of barley to spare, 8 people to house, doth till 16 acres.

John Hakings 30 bushels of barley to sell, 7 people to house, doth till 8 acres.

Richard Tonker 30 bushels of barley to sell, 8 people to house, doth till 8 acres.

Richard Whyte 12 bushels of wheat to sell.

Thomas Even & William Even 10 bushels of wheat to sell, 8 people to house.

Edward Skinner 30 bushels sold to Mr Champnowne not yet delivered & 30 quarters barley yet to sell.

Sum total of wheat 80 bushels of barley ['23' crossed through] 224 bushels

34. Report of Rattery parish, n.d.

PRO, SP14/144/32(xxvii)

Ratterye

A note of all such as have corn ['to sell' crossed through] within our parish and what value and how many people are in their houses and how many acres of land they sow to oats and barley.

Robert Saverye esq. people in his house 30 his corn bushels of wheat one 120, of barley two 100, of oats two hundred bushels, quantity of acres to sow 20 of barley and 35 of oats.

William Helle, vicar, people in his house 10, bushels of wheat 30 and of barley 40 and of oats 40, six acres of barley to sow and five acres of oats.

Gregory Byckford people in his house 14, bushels of wheat 25, of barley 4 score, of oats 120, acres of barley to sow 9 and of oats 20.

Thomas Prowse people in his house 9, bushels of wheat 20 and of barley 30 and of oats 40, acres of oats to sow seven and of barley three.

William Abrahane people in his house 11, bushels of wheat 25 and of barley 30 & of oats 40, acres to sow of oats 9 and of barley five.

Matthew Abraham people in his house 9, bushels of wheat 25 and of barley 30 & of oats 50, acres to sow of barley five and of oats eight.

Alexander Halfe, miller, bought two acres of wheat in the ground & hath 15 bushels of it in his house and hath four people in his house.

The whole sum of wheat is two 265 bushels

the whole sum of barley is 4 400 bushels

the whole sum of oats is 4 400 & 4 score & ten bushels

Thomas Prowse & Robert Luscombe Constables   William Harris Viewer

35. Report of Dittisham parish, n.d.

PRO, SP14/144/32(xxviii)

Couldrige [Coleridge hundred]
Dyttisham

Persons - 18 Ambrose Bellot esq. of wheat bushels - 20
Persons - 6 Ambrose Rupe gent. of barley bushels - 100
Persons - 4 George Rupe gent. of barley bushels - 100
Persons - 20 Thomas Baddefford & John Baddefford of *Capttone* [Capton]
    of wheat bushels - 150
    of barley - 150
    of oats - 150
Persons - 5 Elizabeth Collefford, widow, of wheat and barley - bushels - 15
    of oats - 10
Persons - 4 Nicholas Putt of oats bushels - 20
Persons - 9 William Cristen of wheat bushels - 10
    of barley -10
    of oats -10
William Yabsley of barley bushels - 10
Persons 22 - Adam Lyne of wheat bushels - 10
    of rye -10
    of barley -10
Persons - 8 Henry Austen jun. of wheat & barley - 10
Persons - 4 Ellyzeous Churchward of barley - 15
Persons - 12 John Lech of oats bushels - 12

So we find by our judgement there is to be spared of wheat bushels - 175, of barley - 405, of oats - 210

Constables
John Baddefford
John Leth
Henry Austen jun.

36. Report of South Pool parish, n.d.

PRO, SP14/144/32(xxix)

South *Poole*

A note of the quantity of corn within our parish with the number of persons in each ['mes' crossed through] man's house as followeth:

Mr Doddinge of persons to his house - 15 - of wheat 30 bushels - of barley 80 - of oats 20.

Nicholas Foord of North *Poole* [Pool] persons to his house - 20 - of wheat 100 bushels, of barley 300 - of oats 20.

Nicholas Foord of Scoble - persons 10 - wheat 60 bushels, of barley 500 - of oats 80.

Mr Marten of persons in his house 12- of wheat 30 bushels, of barley 60 bushels.

John Chrispine persons 11 - wheat 30 bushels, of barley 100 - of oats 30.

William Luscombe persons 13 - of wheat 30 bushels - of barley 100 - of oats 60.

William Foord persons 6 - of wheat 8 bushels, of barley 50.

William Sawdon persons 6 - of wheat 00 - of barley 30 bushels.

William Ellett persons 10 - of wheat 20 bushels - of barley 50.

William Garlond persons 8 - of barley 20 bushels.

Andrew Cooke persons 6 - of barley 24 bushels.

Richard Weekes persons 12 - of wheat 6 bushels - of barley 75.

William Randell persons 8 - of wheat 4 - of barley 30.

John Foord persons 8 - of wheat 12 bushels - of barley 12.

Philip Cole persons 8 - of wheat 15 - of barley 32 - oats 20.

Thomas Weekes persons 11 - of barley 20 bushels.

John Edgcombe persons 8 - of wheat 10 - ['30' crossed through] of barley 30.

John Chubbe of Salcombe hath within our parish - of wheat & barley 60 bushels.

Richard Horseman persons 9 - of barley 30 bushels.

The whole quantity of wheat is 415 bushels
> of barley 1563
> of oats 230
>> Total   2208

Constables
[signed] Richard Weekes
[torn. ?Wi]lliam Luscombe
[torn. ?Phi]llip Coll

37. Report of Chivelstone parish, n.d.

PRO, SP14/144/32(xxx)
[endorsed. Elis Edwards band.]

Chevilston
The names of those that can spare corn and grain of this parish 1622.

John Sullocke
of wheat 15 bushels
of barley 40 bushels
of oats 20 bushels
acres to sow 25
people 12

William Predham
of barley 20 bushels
of oats 10 bushels
acres to sow 44
people 10

Peter Collings
of barley 20 bushels
of oats 10 bushels
acres to sow 27
people 12

John Haradon
of barley 18 bushels
of oats 10 bushels
acres to sow 16
people 9

Tamsin Chope
of barley 15 bushels
of oats 15 bushels
people 4

William Chope
of wheat 10 bushels
of barley 8 bushels
of oats 10 bushels
people 12
acres to sow 28

Jasper Chope
of barley 8 bushels
acres to sow 28
people 8

Richard Came
of wheat 22 bushels
of barley 18 bushels
of oats 10 bushels
acres to sow 20
people 10

John Marche
of wheat 8 bushels
of barley 20 bushels
of oats 20 bushels
acres to sow 46

[Th]omas Came
of wheat 14 bushels
[Rich]ard Phillip of barley 8 bushels
[acre]s to sow 8
[peopl]e 9

Edward Snellinge
of ['wheat' crossed through]
barley 8 bushels
 acres to sow 5
people 5

Thomas Ponnd
of wheat 10 bushels
of barley 12 bushels
of oats 6 bushels
acres to sow 20
people 10

Sum 369 bushels

38. Report of Stoke Fleming parish, n.d.

PRO, SP14/144/32(xxxi)

Southfleming
An account of the corn within our parish.

Mr George Pots of wheat 20 bushels, rye an hundred bushels, barley an hundred & fifty bushels, two hundred bushels of oats, he doth plough 30 acres for barley, 20 for oats, his company are 20 persons.

John Page 30 bushels of wheat, of barley one hundred bushels, of oats threescore, he hath 16 acres to be sown unto barley, 8 acres to be sown of oats, his company 12 persons.

Robert Edgcombe forty bushels of wheat, two hundred of barley, he hath 20 acres to be sown to barley, oats 50 bushels, to be sown 8 acres, his company 14 persons.

John Neale six score bushels of barley, he hath 20 acres to be sown, three score bushels of oats, ploughed for oats 10 acres, his company 16 persons.

Henry Neale fifty bushels of wheat, one hundred bushels of barley, ploughed for barley 14 acres, one hundred bushels of oats, ploughed for oats 10 acres, his company 12 persons.

Gilbert Ford two hundred bushels of barley, ploughed for barley 30 acres, of oats three score bushels, ploughed for oats 12 acres, his company 8 persons.

Thomas Luscombe 30 bushels of wheat, of barley six score, ploughed for barley sixteen acres, of oats three score bushels, ploughed for oats 10 acres, his company 11 persons.

Richard Harvy forty bushels of wheat, four score ['bu' crossed through] of barley, ploughed for barley 12 acres, of oats three score bushels, ploughed for oats 8 acres, his company 8 persons.

Roger Oldreeve threescore bushels of barley, ploughed for barley 8 acres, of oats forty bushels, ploughed for oats 6 acres, his company 6 persons.

Robert Wills forty bushels of wheat, fourscore bushels of barley, ploughed for barley 16 acres, of oats fifty bushels, ploughed for oats 10 acres, his company 10 persons.

William Page forty bushels of wheat, of barley six score bushels, ploughed for barley 16 acres, of oats threescore bushels, ploughed for oats 10 acres, his company 11 persons.

The total sum is two thousand 3 hundred and fourscore bushels.

39. Report of Ashprington parish, n.d.

PRO, SP14/144/32(xxxii)
[endorsed. from the county of Devon certificate.]

[torn] which of *Ashbronton* a note of such and [torn] and grain as is to spare.

persons in his house 8

[torn] Sharpham hath to spare
of wheat 20 bushels
of barley 200 bushels   sum 200
of oats 40 bushels   & 80
of peas 20 bushels
he taketh 100 bushels for his own use.

Thomas Lee hath to spare
of wheat 10 bushels   sum 30
of barley 20 bushels
persons in his house 6

Mr Richard Langdon hath to spare
of wheat 20 bushels
of barley 100 bushels   sum 100
of oats 40 bushels   & 60
he taketh 100 bushels for his own
us[e. torn]

John Geast hath to spare
of oats 20 bushels   sum 20
persons in his house

Isaac Pelleton hath to spare
of wheat 10 bushels   sum 30
of barley 15 bushels
of peas 5 bushels
persons in his house 11

Mr Richard Mase hath to spare
of wheat 20 bushels   sum 20

Mary Edmond, widow, hath to spare
of wheat 20 bushels
of barley 20 bushels   sum 80
of oats 40 bushels
persons in her house 12

Charles Badcooke hath to spare
of wheat six bushels   sum 26
of barley 20 bushels
persons in his house 8

John Evlling hath to spare
of barley 10 bushels   sum 30
of oats 20 bushels
persons in his house six

Henry Lee hath to spare
of wheat 10 bushels   sum 24
of barley 10 bushels
of peas 4 bushels
persons in his house 8

Philip Dever hath to spare
of barley 10 bushels   sum 22
of peas 12 bushels
persons in his house 8

Richard Edmond hath to spare
of barley six bushels   s[um] 1[6]
of peas ten bushels
persons in his house 7

William Sharpham hath to spare
of peas 20 bushels
of barley 10 bushels   sum 40
of oats 10 bushels
persons in his house 10

Nicholas Hilley hath to spare
of wheat 10 bushels
of barley 20 bushels   sum 38
of peas 8 bushels

Sum of wheat in all 100 & 32, of
barley 400 & 45, of peas 59, of oats
100 & 70. Sum total is 700 [torn] & six

40. Report of Cornworthy parish, n.d.

PRO, SP14/144/32(xxxiii)

[torn - The na]mes of all those that can spare corn and how many people [?he has - torn] in his houses and how many acres every man doth sow.

James Tockerman hath in his house people 9 and doth sow [acres of - torn] barley and 8 acres of oats and can spare 20 bushels [?of wheat - torn] and hath one hundred bushels of barley and 40 bushels [?of oats - torn].
John Courtas people 9 and doth sow 6 acres of oats and 4 acres of barley and can spare 15 bushels of wheat and hath 60 bushels of barley and hath 22 bushels of oats.
Anstes Howper people 3 and doth sow 6 acres of oats and 2 acres of barley and hath 28 bushels of oats, 26 bushels of barley.
Thomas Yabslie people 7 and doth sow 2 acres of barley hath fifty bushels of barley and can spare 12 bushels of o[ats.]
[torn]ellyan Egford people 7 and doth sow 5 acres of barley and [torn] acres of oats and hath 35 bushels of barley and [torn]50 bushels and can spare 10 bushels of wheat.
Steven Wemoth people 8 and doth sow 8 acres [torn] and 11 acres of oats and 6 acres of peas and [torn] bushels of barley and 60 bushels of oats and 10 bushels [torn].

Mr Richard Reeche hath in Lady Harrice's barton 60 b[ushels - torn] of wheat and 60 bushels of barley and 80 bushels of oats and doth sow three acres of barley and 16 acres of oats.
And what household he hath we know not.

41. Report of Halwell parish, 1623

SP14/144/32(xxxiv)

Devon
The names of those that can spare any corn & grain in the parish of *Hallwell,* their ground being sown. *In the year* 1622.

Imprimis

Samuel Sweete of oats 60 bushels	John Rider of wheat 6 bushels
acres to sow 31	of oats 10 bushels
people 12	acres to sow 23
	people 15

Margaret Lavers of wheat 20 bushels
of rye 10 bushels
of barley 60 bushels
of oats 60 bushels
acres to sow 35
people 14

John Steaphens of wheat 10 bushels
of oats 30 bushels
acres to sow   24
people 10

John Phillips of wheat 5 bushels
of barley 20 bushels
of oats 10 bushels
acres to sow 17
people 12

John Parnell of oats 10 bushels
acres to sow 25
people 16

Nicholas Hyne of wheat 10 bushels
of oats 20 bushels
acres to sow 18
people 11

John Newland of oats 20 bushels
acres to sow 18
people 8

William Newland of wheat 10 bushels
acres to sow 14
people 7

Leonard Wadland of wheat 20 bushels
of barley 20 bushels
of oats 40 bushels
acres to sow 18
people 8

Richard Pecke of wheat 30 bushels
of oats 20 bushels
acres to sow 20
people 12

Roger Earle of barley 10 bushels
of oats 10 bushels
acres to sow 15
people 12

Nicholas Lee of barley 30
acres to sow 10
people 2

John Penhey of wheat 10 bushels
of oats 10 bushels
acres to sow 10
people 3

John Luscome of rye 4 bushels
of oats 15 bushels
of barley 8 bushels
people 3

The sum	bushels
of wheat	1 - 2 - 1 [121]
of barley	1 - 4 - 8 [148]
of rye	0 - 1 - 4 [14]
of oats	3 - 1 - 5 [315]

Total sum 598

42. Certificate. Justices of South Molton, North Tawton and Witheridge hundreds to the High Sheriff of Devon, 28 February 1623.

PRO, SP14/144/32(1)

Mr Sheriff,
We his Majesty's Justices of Peace dwelling within the hundreds of Southmolton, North Tawton & Witheridge in this county of Devon being a subdivision allotted to the care of the Justices dwelling within the same, at our late general meeting for that behalf, do in obedience of his Majesty's late proclamation and Orders therewith enjoined make certificate. That we the said Justices did in the beginning of the month of February last past (which was so soon as we received the said proclamation & Orders) direct our precepts unto the high constable of the said hundreds to cause the under constables & other honest & substantial inhabitants within the said hundreds to the number of thirty from each hundred & upwards to appear before us at *Chulmeley* [Chulmleigh] some ten days following, with instructions to the said high constables as by the said Orders we are directed who appeared accordingly ['bef' crossed through] before us (saving some five parishes within the hundred of Northtawton who through the negligence & carelessness of Nicholas Davye one of the head constables of the said hundred being within his division appeared not but together with himself made default) to whom we did declare & give charge according to the said Orders, who some ten days then following delivered us their presentments, whereof we having taken due consideration did forthwith give order accordingly for the weekly bringing into the market of such quantity of corn & other grain as we conceived proportionable to every man's store thereof according to our instructions mentioned in the said Orders. The markets within our subdivision being South Molton & *Chulmeleigh* are yet plentifully furnished with corn & other grain at reasonable prices, *vizt* wheat 9s 6d, rye 7s 4d, oats 2s 2d & oaten malt 2s 8d, beans and barley agree not with our grounds & therefore we have little thereof grown in those parts. Our measure here is twelve gallons. We have suppressed the number of malsters & alehouses and have & will pursue the rest of the said Orders with our best endeavours given under our hands at *Chulmeleigh* the last of February 1622 [1623].
Your very loving friends,
[signed] Edward Chichester Lewis Pollarde Humphry Bury John Wood

43. Certificate. Justices of Crediton, West Budleigh and part of Wonford hundreds to the High Sheriff of Devon, 15 March 1623.

PRO, SP14/144/32(iii)
[endorsed. to the right worshipful the high Sheriff of the county of Devon.]

Mr Sheriff,
We his Majesty's Justices of peace dwelling within the hundreds of Crediton, West Budleigh and *Wonnford* West in this county of Devon being a subdivision allotted to the care of the said Justices dwelling within the said hundreds do in obedience to his Majesty's late proclamation and Orders therein enjoined make our second certificate in this behalf. That we the said Justices have found the corn and other grains within the market of Crediton to be of the prices following, *vizt* wheat at 7s 6d the bushel, rye at 6s, barley at 4s 8d, barley malt at 4s 10d, peas at 6s and beans at 5s and some or one of us have ordinarily attended the said market of Crediton every market day whereby the poor people have been by means thereof provided of corn by our proclamations somewhat under the price of the said market to their reasonable contentments and will and still do pursue the rest of the said orders with our best endeavours given under our hands this 15th of March 1622 [1623].
[signed] John Northcott   Richard Reynell   John Davie   Edward Cotton

44. Letter. High Sheriff of Cornwall to the Privy Council, 3 May 1623.

PRO, SP14/144/10
[endorsed. To the right honourable my very good Lords the Lords of his Majesty's most Honourable Privy Council.
Certificate about corn from Penheale in *Cornwale* 3 of May 1623.]

Right honourable,
My most humble duty remembered. I have according to your honour's late directions for the preventing of the great and excessive prices of corn in the county of Cornwall in this present time of dearth and scarcity made known unto all the Justices of Peace in the said county the tenor of your honour's Orders and instructions prescribed touching the premises, and herewith I humbly present unto your Honours those certificates which I have received from some of the Justices which are for four hundreds only, namely, for the Hundreds of Lesnewth, Trigg, Penwith and *Kirry* [Kerrier]. And from the Justices of the rest of the hundreds, being five other hundreds, namely the hundreds of East, West, Stratton, *Pider* [Pydar] and Powder, I have not as yet received any certificates from them which is the cause I have so long deferred this my certificate unto

your Honours wherein I humbly submit myself unto your Honourable considerations. And so in all duty I rest, at your honours' service to be commanded,
[signed] John Speccott

From Penheale in Cornwall the third of May 1623

45. Certificate. Justices of Lesnewth hundred to the High Sheriff of Cornwall, 13 March 1623.

PRO, SP14/144/10(i)
[endorsed. To the right worthy our very loving friend Sir John Speccot knight, High Sheriff of the county of *Cornewall* these deliver.
March 1623 from *Lanceston* touching corn.]

Hundred of Lesnewth

Right worthy sir,
According to the Orders sent down there hath been a sufficient jury returned for the viewing of the corn within every parish and upon the return thereof it appeareth that there is great want of corn to supply one market of *Botreax Castle* [Boscastle] within the hundred of Lesnewth, and every market day there is order taken by the Justices to observe the Orders appointed. Now the price in the said market is of wheat double Winchester measure 12s & of barley 7s 6d & of oats 3s for no other corn cometh to that market. This is all can be certified for this time but it is feared that the price will grow still more & more, & the rather because upon this view the great want is known. Thus craving pardon we take our leave ever resting, at your disposal,
[signed] William Parker John Wooth James Maryngton

Launceston 13 *March* 1622 [1623]

46. Certificate. Justices of Trigg hundred to the High Sheriff of Cornwall, 13 March 1623.

PRO, SP14/144/10(ii)
[endorsed. To the right worthy our very loving friend Sir John Speccot knight High Sheriff of the county of *Cornewall* these deliver.]

Hundred of Trigg

Right worthy sir,
According to the Orders sent down, there hath been a sufficient jury returned
for the viewing of the corn within every parish within the hundred of *Trig*, and
upon the return thereof it appeareth that there is great want of corn to supply one
market of *Bodmyn* within the said hundred and every market day there is order
taken by the Justices to observe the Orders appointed. Now the price in the said
market is of wheat double Winchester measure 12s and of barley 7s 6d, and of
oats 3s, for no other corn cometh to the market. This is all can be certified for
this time, but it is feared that the price will grow still more and more, & the
rather because upon this view the great want is known. Thus craving pardon
we take our leave ever resting, at your disposal,
[signed] Reginald Mohun William Parker

Launceston 13 *March* 1622 [1623]

47. Certificate. Justices of Penwith and Kerrier hundreds to the High Sheriff of Cornwall, 1 April 1623.

PRO, SP14/144/10(iii)
[endorsed. *Penwth and Kirr.*]

First April 1623
Hundred of Penwith & Kirry

According to the Lords' directions there hath been a sufficient jury returned for
the viewing of the corn of every parish within the Hundreds of *Penwth & Kirr:*
and upon their relation it appeareth there is like to be great want of corn to
supply the markets in these hundreds which are four every market day & there
is order taken by us, to observe the directions appointed. Now the prices in
these makets are, of wheat double Winchester measure 12s, of barley 7s and of
oats 7s 8d for no other grain comes to our markets. This is all we can certify
for this time but it is feared the price will daily increase, if foreign parts help
us not.
[signed] Francis Godolphin Arthur Harris John Seyntaubyn John Trefusis

The Certificate of the Justices within the Hundreds of *Penwth & Kirr* concerning
the corn business according to the Lords' directions therin.

48. Letter. High Sheriff of Devon to the Privy Council, 10 May 1623.

PRO, SP14/144/32

May it please your Lordships to be advertised,
That wheareas I have received a proclamation with Orders of directions appointed by his Majesty for the preventing & remedying of the dearth of corn & other grain in this county. The Justices of the Peace within this county have assembled themselves together according to his Majesty's directions and have called before them the high constables, petty constables and other honest persons within their several divisions to view the corn & to see the execution of these orders. And that the said Justices have certified unto me being Sheriff of the county of Devon their proceedings according to his Majesty's instructions. All which certificates I return up unto your Lordships as by the Book of Orders I am commanded. So reccomending my service unto your Lordships I humbly take my leave and rest, your Lordships' ready to be commanded,
[signed] Edmund Fortescue, Sheriff

Exon the 10th of May 1623

49. Certificate. Justices of South Molton, Witheridge and North Tawton hundreds to the High Sheriff of Devon, 11 April 1623.

PRO, SP14/144/32(ii)

Mr Sheriff,
We his Majesty's justices of the peace dwelling within the hundreds of Southmolton, *Witherridge* and North tawton in this county of Devon, do in obedience to his Majesty's late proclamation and Orders make ['or' crossed through] our second certificate in this behalf that we the said justices do find the price of corn to lessen somewhat in our markets - *vizt* wheat 9s, rye 7s, oats 2s & oaten malt 2s 8d. We cannot yet understand of any that do keep back their corn from the markets or that have shown any other contempt against his Majesty's said Orders which Orders we will still carefully pursue with our best endeavours given under our hands this 11th of April 1623.
Your very loving friends,
[signed] Edward Chichester Lewis Pollarde Humphrey Bury John Wood

50. Certificate. Justices of Crediton, West Budleigh and part of Wonford hundreds to the High Sheriff of Devon, 24 April 1623.

PRO, SP14/144/32(iv)
[endorsed. To the right worshipful the high Sheriff of the county of Devon.]

We his Majesty's Justices of the peace dwelling within the hundreds of Crediton, West *Budley* and *Woundford* West in this county of Devon (being a sub-division allotted to the care of the Justices dwelling within the said hundreds) do in obedience to his Majesty's late proclamation and Orders therein enjoined make our third certificate, that the market is yet reasonably served with corn and grain at the prices following *vizt*, wheat 9s the bushel, rye 6s, barley 5s, pease 6s, beans 4s 4d and barley malt 5s. And that we be still careful to suppress malsters, forestallers, engrossers and regraters and others the causes of dearth, according to his said Majesty's Proclamation and Orders, given under our hands this 24th of April 1623.
[signed] John Northcot   Edward Cotton   Richard Reynell   John Davie

51. Certificate. Justices of Black Torrington, Hartland and two other hundreds[2] to the Privy Council, n.d.[3]

PRO, SP14/138/116
[endorsed. To the right honourable the Lords and others of his Majesty's most honourable Privy Council deliver these.]

Right honourables,
Our duties in all humble manner remembered may it please you to be informed that according to the King's Majesty's express command in a certain Book lately set forth for the mitigation of the high price of corn and grain & divers Orders therein contained to be put in due execution we accordingly to our duties have done our best endeavours to the performance of every clause in the said Book required to be done: all such corn as every inhabitant can spare is by us ordered in fit and due proportion within our division consisting of 4 hundreds and about 64 parishes to be weekly brought into the next adjoining markets until the 16th of August next we find by the presentments of the viewers of corn and grain that the corn and grain within these parts will not be sufficient to supply the wants of the people. The quantity of corn to be spared within these parishes of all sorts of grain are of wheat 2007 bushels, of barley 1440 bushels, of rye 669 bushels, of oats 5239 bushels, of malt 356 bushels, of peas 160 bushels. And the price of each of them by the bushel being nearer about 12 gallons in every market within this division is for wheat 10s 6d, barley 6s, rye 7s, oats 2s 6d, malt 2s 8d, peas 9s, concerning tipplers we find (unless such as dwell in town) their poverty to be such as divers of them have given over the

same. For badgers, kiddiers, broggers or carriers of corn there are none in these parts. His Majesty's command in the Book requireth us to certify your honours herewith which we leave to your Lords in consideration. And do in all duty and ['ha' crossed through] humbleness take our leave and remain, at your Lordships' commandments,
[signed] Nicholas Prydeaux John Arscott Dunsland Nicholas Luttrell

1. It is likely that this survey was taken inFebruary 1623: (**33**).

2. There is no identification made on the survey but these signatures must be of John Arscott of Dunsland (Bradford parish), Nicholas Prideaux of Thuborough (Sutcombe parish) and Nicholas Luttrell of Hartland Abbey (Hartland parish).

3. The certificate is undated but must be from the enquiries following the harvest failure of 1622, and not that of 1630, because Nicholas Prideaux died in 1628. I am grateful to Mary Wolffe for this information.

THE HARVEST FAILURE OF 1630

52. Letter. Justices of West hundred[1] to the Privy Council, 9 November 1630.

PRO, SP16/175/35
[endorsed. To the right honourable the Lords of his Majesty's most honourable Privy Council, these deliver.
22 of November. From the Lord Mohun and John Bastard, Justices of the Peace of the county of Cornwall, about engrossers of corn.]

Our duties in most humble manner remembered,
May it please your honours to be advertised that whereas we lately received command by his Majesty's proclamation and Book of instructions for restraining of forestallers, engrossers and unlawful buyers of corn, as also to prevent the converting of so much barley into malt, we have used our best endeavours by calling the country before us and acquainting them with his Majesty's command therein. And we are credibly informed that there have been (before the receipt of his Majesty's proclamation) carried away out of our county very great quantity of corn, of wheat about 5000 bushels, besides barley and oats, which have caused a great dearth in our country and is likely daily to increase if those engrossers of corn be not speedily prevented. And amongst the rest we have taken notice of one Richard Snellinge and Thomas Seallinge of Plymouth to be offenders in this kind having bought great quantities of corn before the same was brought into open market. And therefore we have thought good to bind them to appear before your honours whose confessions and recognizances we herewith present you, leaving the same unto your honours' wisdoms to dispose of and ourselves ready in all duty to observe your commands.
[signed] Reginald Mohun Joseph Bastayd

Hall this 9th of November 1630

47

53. Examination of Richard and Thomas Snelling, Plymouth brewers, 3 November 1630.

PRO, SP16/175/35(i)

Cornewall

The examination of Richard Snellinge ['Bre' crossed through] of Plymouth in the county of Devon, brewer, taken at Pelynt the third of November 1630 before Sir Reginald Mohun, knight and baronet, and Joseph Bastard, esq., two of his Majesty's Justices of the Peace within the said county of *Cornewall*.

Sayeth that he hath bought about one thousand bushels of corn in the county of *Cornewall* of divers persons there before the said was brought into the market. Whereof 500 bushels are at *Mevagessie* [Mevagissey], 200 bushels at Fowey and 300 bushels are at Ruan Lanihorne ready to be brought by water to Plymouth.

[signed] Reginald Mohun   Joseph Bastayd

The examination of Thomas Sneallinge of Plymouth, brewer, taken the day and year abovesaid.

Sayeth that he and his servants by his directions have bought near about five hundred bushels of barley and wheat in the county of *Cornewall* of several persons there before the same was brought into any markets.

[signed] Reginald Mohun   Joseph Bastayd

54. Recognizance of Richard and Thomas Snelling, Plymouth brewers, 3 November 1630.

PRO, SP16/175/35(ii)

Cornwall. Recognizances taken at Pelynt the third day of November 6 Charles 1, King of England etc. before Reginald Mohun, knight and baronet, and Joseph Bastard, esq., justices of the peace of the King.

Richard Snellinge of Plymouth in the county of Devon, brewer, acknowledges that he owes to the said Lord the King £200 to be raised from goods, chattels, lands and tenements.

Thomas Snealinge of Plymouth aforesaid, brewer, acknowledges that he owes to the said Lord the King £100 of legal money to be raised from his goods, chattels, lands and tenements.

Under this condition that the self same Richard and Thomas personally appear

before the Council of the Lord the King on the 20th day of November next
following and there and then respond to all those who object to them.
[signed] Reginald Mohun Joseph Bastayd

55. Reasons for and against the transportation of Cornish corn to Plymouth.

PRO, SP16/175/35(iii)

The reasons that the engrossers & forestallers of corn do give are these.
First, they say that it is for the provision of the shipping of Plymouth for their new found land voyage.
And answer there unto
First, their shipping may be provided for with corn and all other neccesaries in their own country in Devon being plentiful with ten times more than they are to use therein.Then they have no course to come into *Cornewall* for such provision, we being hardly able to relieve our own country and furnish our shipping in the like voyage and also for our Ireland fishing and in the deeps and at the [St Michaels's] Mount and other places of fishing.
Next we answered, that their new found land voyages do no good to this country for it taketh away all or the most part of the salt that our country should use, which maketh such a dearth thereof that where it was sold for 2s or 3s a bushel it is now sold for 14s a bushel, by means whereof the people cannot have [the] wherewith[all] to save their flesh & fish for their relief. So now the poor must either be enforced to use unlawful means to relieve themselves or else endure great famine & misery.
Also, the Newfoundland shipping do sell their fish there in that country to strangers or to such as transport the same to foreign nations, and bring home but small quantities thereof, by means whereof they sell it here now for 14s a hundred, when always heretofore it was not sold above 7s 6d the hundred.

Corn - Concerning corn, whereas it was within there 3 months past sold for 6s a bushel it is now at 12s the bushel in regards of such engrossing & forestalling of corn and is very likely every day to be dearer, if it be not saved, for the cry of the poor is so lamentable, as it will grieve any man to hear it.
Also, there hath been engrossed & transported away from *Padstowe* & other ports out of *Cornewall* within these 3 months past (before the restraint came) five thousand bushels of wheat & barley at least, by *Bristowe* [Bristol] men, whose names we cannot yet learn.

56. Petition. Thomas Stephens, Richard Snelling and other bakers and brewers to the Privy Council, n.d.[2]

PRO, SP16/175/116

The Bakers & Brewers of Plymouth.
To the right honourable the Lords & others of his Majesty's most honourable Privy Council.
The humble petition of Thomas Stephens, Richard Snelling & others, bakers and brewers of Plymouth.
Showing
That heretofore the petitioners have supplied his Majesty's ships with great quantities of bread and beer, which now by reason of the scarcity of corn there, they are unable to do if occasion should happen.
And for the further supply of the said service and of the fishing trade (by which that part of this kingdom is only relieved) they have bought certain quantities of corn in *Cornewall* which they cannot bring thence without order from your Lordships.
They therefore must humbly beseech your Lordship's to grant them warrant for the removing of the said corn from *Cornewall* to Plymouth they putting in sufficient security not to transport it to any other place.
And the petitioners will daily pray for your Lordships .

57. Certificate of Justices of Pydar hundred, 2 December 1630.

PRO, SP16/176/13
[endorsed. 2nd December 1630. A certificate of Inquiry.]

Cornwall - *hundred of Pider*
          A certificate by Inquirers of the number of persons which are in the houses of every householder of the several parishes together with the quantity of the bushels of corn & grain of every inhabitant within the said hundred the bushel containing twenty gallons and what corn every inhabitant is to sow this year to come and also what every malster, baker, brewer & tippler do malt, bake & brew weekly within the several parishes of the said hundred. And what corn & grain hath been sold by any person or persons out of the markets since the last harvest and to whom. And the prices taken at *St Cullumb* [St Columb Major] the second day of December 1630. Before us Edward Coswarth & John Prideaux, esquires, two of his Majesty's Justices of the Peace within the county aforesaid as follows.

(57a) *parish of St Breocke* [Breock]

	Persons	Wheat bushels	Barley bushels	Barley tillage	Oats tillage none	Oats none
John Prideaux esq.	20	40	80	40		
Nicholas Tredenicke, gent.	11	20	50	15		
John Hocker	18	60	50	16		
Roger Weary	18	60	80	16		
George Randle	10	30	20	7		
Henry May	10	30	50	11		
Thomas Beare, gent.	0	20	30	4		
William Weary	16	30	40	12		
Nicholas Daudye	10	40	50	10		
Balthaser Parnel	7	20	20	4		
Richard Rickard	3	20	30	5		
Richard Hicks	10	45	35	10		
John Wearye	0	60	60	10		
Charles Hocker	13	40	40	10		
James Braban	9	25	20	9		
William Moone	0	30	0	0		
Christopher Francke	9	40	35	9		
Samuel Harvey	13	25	30	6		
William Daudy	7	40	45	9		
Marian Richards, *widow*	6	40	40	12		
Francis Lukey	12	35	30	7		
William Lukey	0	30	25	3		
Francis Grigg	10	20	20	8		
John Harvey	14	100	60	12		
Sampson Biscomb	5	40	30	6		
Richard Harvey	0	25	0	0		
Christian Gullyn, *widow*	12	30	30	4		
Robert Blake	16	50	80	12		
Dorothy Wilton, *widow*	12	60	24	16		
Robert Daudye	6	40	70	12		
John Pedler	14	15	30	7		
Peter Blake, clerk	8	30	30	7		
Anthony Woolcocke	6	25	20	6		
Margaret Blake, *widow*	3	30	20	4		
John Blake	15	40	50	18		
Christopher Levitopp	15	40	50	12		
George Handford	5	20	0	0		
Richard Morrishe	5	40	30	8		
Arthur Blake	9	50	35	8		

(57b)   Breock cont'd

Christopher Pedler & his mother	13	80	70	16
Nicholas Billinge	10	20	15	40
James Typper	2	20	20	4
Reginald Blake	4	10	20	2
David Blake	5	10	10	3
Francis Marshall	6	10	15	4
Richard Band	9	15	20	4
Burcott Pethygrewe	14	20	30	8
John Woolcocke	0	15	25	5

Sum total of wheat ['1318' crossed through] 1,635 bushels, of barley ['1606' crossed through] 1800 bushels.

parish of Padestowe [Padstow]

	Persons	wheat bushels	barley bushels	barley tillage	oats bushels	tillage of oats none
John Prideaux, gent.	8	46	40	0	0	
Thomas Martyn	8	40	40	0	0	
Nyott Doutt	9	16	0	0	0	
John Tom	14	0	100	5	0	
Gregory Stribley	21	100	600	50	0	
John French	4	240	0	0	0	
William Jolly	12	50	60	20	0	
Jane Blake, *widow*	9	20	-	-		
Thomasine Parking, *widow*	4	10	50	8	0	
Richard Lukey	16	16	16	0	0	
Edmund Land	14	8	5	0	0	
William Emott	12	8	6	0	0	
James Cundye	6	12	15	0	0	
Justas Marsh	6	20	60	6	0	
John Warne	15	60	0	0	0	
John Martyn	9	40	150	20	20	
Jonathan Tubb	3	25	60	20	0	
George Warne	0	25	30	0	0	
Walter Rounsevall	5	8	30	0	0	
Thomas Rounsevall	0	90	70	0	0	
Peter Pedcocke	5	0	30	4	0	
Henry Peter	8	60	8	10	0	
Gregory Warne	8	30	80	14	0	
Petrocke Martyn	4	15	30	6	0	

(57c)

Peter Trelingst	3	0	25	3	0
John Peter	16	40	80	23	0
John Arthur	16	60	120	16	0
Thomas & William Arthur	0	50	80	10	0
Stephen Parken	18	90	100	16	40b
Peter Martyn	8	20	70	15	0
Robert Glover	8	16	16	7	0
John Carne	4	26	15	6	0
Stephen Best	6	20	30	6	0
Richard Rounsevall	16	80	60	0	0

Sum total of wheat 1,318 bushels, of barley 1,606 bushels, of oats 60 bushels.

St Issey *parish*	Persons	Wheat bushels	Barley bushels	Bushels of oats	Barley to be tilled	oats to be tilled
John Hocken	15	30	15	40	4	10
Martin Hocken	5	15	15	20	7	3
Martin Tom	0	20	20	0	7	0
John Warne	7	20	20	0	10	0
Thomas Pearse	14	30	40	0	14	0
William Lobb	7	30	50	0	8	0
Arter Stribbly	0	80	50	0	16	0
William Cornishe	8	10	50	0	9	0
Digory Udy	14	30	40	0	17	0
Gilbert Bligh	12	70	70	0	12	0
Dorothy Cornishe, *widow*	11	50	30	0	20	0
John Morcomb	10	50	50	0	9	0
John Bettie	8	60	20	0	15	0
John Pearse	4	10	40	0	7	0
Richard Kent	12	40	30	0	13	0
Henry Penaliggan	6	15	40	0	9	0
Robert Sandowe	9	30	40	0	7	0
Nicholas Warne	13	90	50	0	20	0
John Rowse	0	40	0	0	0	0
John Arthur	10	50	40	10	10	0
Digory Arthur	14	60	40	10	12	0
John Pryn	12	90	40	0	10	0
Francis Hockyn	15	50	40	0	11	0

Sum total of wheat 1000/ 10 bushels, of barley 800/ 30 bushels, of oats 80 bushels.

(57d)   St Merryn *parish*

	Persons	Wheat bushels	Barley bushels		Bushels of oats	
Henry Michell, gent.	30	100	200	0	60	0
Nicholas Leach	0	180	300	0	0	0
John Michell, gent.	10	60	65	0	25	0
Richard Jenkinge	8	12	50	0	20	0
Thomas Jeffry	12	60	60	0	25	0
Nicholas Oliver	4	16	16	0	0	0
John Martyn	9	80	100	0	30	0
William Bennett	6	0	50	0	0	0
Richard Vivian	10	20	60	0	16	0
Drewe Withiell	9	20	70	0	18	0
William Ivy	5	6	20	0	6	0
John Ivy	20	12	50	0	16	0
Thomas Speare	11	20	80	0	16	0
John Weary	12	30	60	0	30	0
William Williams	18	50	70	0	24	0
John Sibly, gent.	0	60	50	0	0	0
Pollodor Juell & Richard Lukey	0	0	100	0	0	0

Sum total of wheat 700/ 46 bushels, of barley 1,491.

Callomb [St Columb] Minor *parish*

	persons	bushels of wheat	bushels of barley	bushels of oats	acres of barley to be tilled	acres of oats to be tilled
Thomas Mundy	40	150	300	40	40	12
John Mundy, gent.	30	60	60	30	20	10
John Watts	28	250	150	80	20	18
John Symon	12	80	60	30	10	10
Robert Carne	16	60	80	60	10	6
Henry Cooke	14	60	80	30	10	6
Roger Jllerye	10	40	40	12	8	5
John Whitford	11	110	60	40	10	8
Thomas Cocke	10	50	5	30	6	5
Thomas Martyn	16	100	50	20	8	4
William Watts	12	40	10	30	5	5
John Sampson	10	120	80	60	16	8
John Roberts jun.	8	50	100	20	5	4

(57e)

William Benny	12	60	40	40	7	7
Thomas Dooble	9	60	16	16	2	2
Edward Cock	10	40	40	20	7	5
Thomas John	9	30	20	20	3	4
William Symon	13	50	60	20	7	6
Richard Jenking	10	30	40	3	0	0
Richard Stone	9	30	100	20	14	5
Roger Harvy	7	30	30	10	4	3
John Cock	14	60	40	20	4	3
Leonard Budlye	10	30	50	20	6	4
John Bonython, gent.	14	40	26	5	0	0
Richard Boundye	10	50	30	30	6	6
Edward Ruell	4	30	40	7	0	0
Cullan Quintrill	9	30	20	30	6	7
William Hamblyn	9	15	20	8	5	3
Melchezedeck Rawlyn	6	30	30	10	6	6
John Townsend	7	20	0	1	0	0
Thomas Kestle	3	10	16	10	0	0
John Jenking	9	20	0	0	0	0
John Roberts sen.	8	20	16	14	6	2
Julian Roberts, *widow*	7	30	20	0	3	0
John Sparke	6	20	16	8	2	1
Thomas Symon	0	0	20	0	0	0

Sum total of wheat 1,995, of barley 1,900 bushels.

Newland [**Newlyn East**] *parish*

	Persons	Bushels of wheat	Bushels of barley	Bushels of oats	Acres of barley to be tilled	Acres of oats to be tilled
Nicholas Burlace	7	30	20	6	0	0
Alexander Daniel	15	40	20	40	0	0
Thomas Pelean	8	30	0	20	8	0
Joane Gibbs, *widow*	8	20	10	30	8	0
Nicholas Warren	12	20	12	20	9	0
Stephen Kest	10	20	20	12	4	0
Thomas Trebarhan	4	20	0	12	0	6
John Asble	8	20	0	20	0	7
John Hodg	6	10	10	0	5	0
John Androwe	7	20	20	12	0	6

(57f)   **Newlyn East cont'd**

William Gibbs	9	20	20	0	5	0
William Wills	0	20	0	0	0	0
Thomas Colmer, clerk	0	30	0	0	0	0
James Elvans	0	20	0	0	0	0
Enoder Gullye	0	30	0	0	0	0

Sum total of wheat 350 bushels, of barley 124 bushels, of oats ['17'crossed through] 172 bushels.

parish of Cubart [Cubert]

	Persons	Bushels of wheat	Bushels of barley	Bushels of oats	Acres of barley to be tilled	Acres of oats to be tilled
John Prideaux, gent.	20	40	70	20	20	0
John Davyes	20	80	80	0	14	0
John Androwe	18	40	60	0	18	0
John Griggor	12	30	40	0	7	0
William Chenowth	12	30	30	0	5	0
Sampson Treglenack	7	30	40	0	5	0
Bennet Androwe	9	40	30	0	7	0
William Maie	10	40	40	0	6	0
Jane Carvolth, *widow*	6	30	30	0	4	0
William Penrose	9	30	30	0	5	0
Bennett Bennett	8	30	40	0	5	0
Joane Hodge, *widow*	4	40	40	0	5	0
John Hodg	9	15	40	0	7	0
William Carvolth	11	40	30	0	7	0
Pascowe Penrose	4	18	30	0	3	0

Sum total of wheat 533 bushels, of barley 630 bushels.

parish of Crantocke [Crantock]

	Persons	Bushels of wheat	Bushels of barley	Bushels of oats	Acres of barley to be tilled	Acres of oats to be tilled
Thomas Vivian	10	30	30	0	4	0
Ephraim Skinner	8	15	15	0	2	0
Elizabeth Nicoll, *widow*	5	12	0	0	12	0

(57g)

Savorye Androwe	12	60	20	12	3	0
Richard Bligh	3	60	40	0	6	0
James Elwance	12	30	24	0	6	0
Henry James	3	20	12	10	2	0
William Huddye	10	60	40	0	7	0
Robert Clemowe	10	90	30	40	8	0
Sampson Dungye	7	50	40	20	8	0
Henry Stephens	8	70	60	12	10	0
Digory Vivian	15	80	60	12	16	0
Thomas Symons	2	40	40	0	10	0
Mr Lovie	12	40	60	0	20	0
John Michell	8	35	35	0	6	0
Leonard Browne, gent	12	40	60	0	20	0
Edward Rillston	8	12	30	0	9	0
Nicholas Eare	7	20	20	0	6	0

Sum total of wheat 759 bushels, of barley 631 bushels, of oats 106.

Enodor [St Enoder] *parish*

	Persons	Bushels of wheat	Bushels of barley	Bushels of oats	Acres of barley to be tilled	Acres of oats to be tilled
Francis Gulley	17	80	20	120	6	20
Zachary Arundle	20	40	20	40	10	14
Joseph Jollye	16	40	80	40	10	12
William Trevethicke	7	40	50	40	8	10

Sum total of wheat 200 bushels, of barley 170 bushels, of oats 240 bushels.

parish of Lanivett [Lanivet]

	Persons	Bushels of wheat	Bushels of barley	Bushels of oats	Acres of barley to be tilled	Acres of oats to be tilled
Richard Courtney, esq.	30	80	40	100	0	0
Francis Courtney, gent.	16	30	30	40	0	0
Andrew Fenton, gent.	11	25	0	40	0	0
Thomas Wyett, gent.	12	40	10	60	0	0

(57h)   Lanivet cont'd

John Wymond, gent.	12	40	35	60	0	0
Elizabeth Jenking, *widow*	40	30	50	0	0	
Richard Bullocke	9	40	20	50	0	0
Thomas Hicks	8	30	20	50	0	0
Richard Collyns	10	25	20	30	0	0
John Drewe	7	24	16	50	0	0
Nicholas Hawkyn	14	34	20	60	0	0
Christopher Greene	8	25	0	30	0	0
Winifrid Avery, *widow*	20	0	30	0	0	
Jolme Collyns, *widow*	10	20	15	30	0	0

Sum total of wheat 473 bushels, of barley 256 bushels, of oats 680 bushels.

Perran Zabula [Perranzabuloe] *parish*

	Persons	Bushels of wheat	Bushels[1] of barley	Bushels of oats	Acres of barley to be tilled	Acres of oats to be tilled
Vesula Colmer, *widow*	24	20	20	0	10	0
John Hockyn	10	5	5	0	10	0
Thomas May	11	10	10	0	10	0
Christopher Hendra	11	15	15	0	10	0
Thomas Resugga	7	0	0	0	12	0
Stephen Cotty	8	6	6	0	6	0
John Roberts	6	10	10	0	10	0
John Jenkins	4	5	5	0	5	0
Christopher Williams	8	6	6	0	7	0
John Battyon	5	6	6	0	6	0
Christopher Cardoll	1	5	5	0	4	0

Sum total of wheat 84 bushels, of barley 84 bushels.

Mawgan[-in-Pydar] *parish*

	Persons	Bushels of wheat	Bushels of barley	Bushels of oats	Acres of barley to be tilled	Acres of oats to be tilled
Rosecleere Arscott	30	80	60	40	20	9
Richard Pears	30	160	100	100	20	20

(57i)

William Noy, esq.	0	36	8	12	0	0
Edward Tregennowe	12	30	40	0	7	0
Thomas Bennett	25	130	150	10	13	5
Gilbert Cayser	10	50	60	0	9	3
William Benny	12	60	60	0	7	0
Mawgan Hendra	12	50	12	18	7	3
Oates George	2	15	50	0	10	0
Thomas Howse	8	30	30	20	5	6
Martin Jolly	0	20	10	10	4	0
James Bennett	0	0	80	0	8	
Robert Jllary	0	60	100	0	0	0

Sum total of wheat 661 bushels, of barley 672 bushels, 290 bushels of oats.

St Agnes *parish*

	Persons	Bushels of wheat	Bushels of barley	Bushels of oats	Acres of barley to be tilled	Acres of oats to be tilled
John Crocker	12	10	0	0	0	0

Sum wheat 10 bushels.

St Wenn *parish*

	Persons	Bushels of wheat	Bushels of barley	Bushels of oats	Acres of barley to be tilled	Acres of oats to be tilled
John Typpett	18	30	30	100	6	20
Henry May	4	60	20		6	20
John Chappell	8	15	20	30	4	4
Christopher Best	24	90	30	100	8	26
Maximilian Cocke	10	4	30	60	6	16
John Silly gent.	26	70	40	150	0	0
John ['Cock' crossed through] Coade	18	40		50	0	15
Dorothy Parking	10	20	12	30	4	10
Grace Chappell	7	15	0	30	3	6
William Coade	17	50	50	50	8	16

(57j)   St Wenn cont'd

Ralph Udy	12	40	30	6	5	10
Grace Bakyn, *widow*	14	20	15	30	5	12

Sum of wheat 454 bushels, of barley 377 bushels, of oats 646 bushels.

Withiell [Withiel] *parish*

	Persons	Bushels of wheat	Bushels of barley	Bushels of oats	Acres of barley to be tilled	Acres of oats to be tilled
James Bonython	16	12	12	10	0	0
Richard Moyle	0	25	0	0	0	0
Richard Mapowder	10	20	0	20	0	0
John Williams	0	4	50	20	0	0

Sum total of wheat 63 bushels, of barley 62 bushels, of oats 50 bushels.

Lanhidrock [Lanhydrock] *parish*

	Persons	Bushels of wheat	Bushels of barley	Bushels of oats	Acres of barley to be tilled	Acres of oats to be tilled
Thomas Bullocke	8	20	0	6	16	30
John Sarvis	11	6	0	5	2	7
Francis Hockyn	4	4	0	6	2	5

Sum total of wheat 30 bushels, of barley none, of oats 17 bushels.

St *Evall* [Eval] *parish*

	Persons	Bushels of wheat	Bushels of barley	Bushels of oats	Acres of barley to be tilled	Acres of oats to be tilled
John Robbyns	21	60	120	80	20	20
Thomas Trebethick	9	30	60	0	12	0
Simon Leach	12	40	150	0	20	0

(57k)

Nicholas John	9	15	50	0	7	0
Robert Arter	7	40	70	0	12	0
Thomas Brynn	10	20	30	0	5	0
William Gybbs	4	6	30	0	4	0

Sum total of wheat 2,011 bushels, of barley 510 bushels, of oats 80 bushels.

St Ervan *parish*

	Persons	Bushels of wheat	Bushels of barley	Bushels of oats	Acres of barley to be tilled	Acres of oats to be tilled
Richard Lanyon	0	30	50	40	0	0
John Coad, clerk	4	40	4	40	0	0
Richard Pears	0	80	0	0	0	0
John Tom	18	40	50	0	20	0
Humphry Arter	6	20	40	0	8	0

Sum total of wheat 210 bushels, of barley 140 bushels, of oats 80 bushels.

parish of St Collomb [Columb] **Major**

	Persons	Bushels of wheat	Bushels of barley	Bushels of oats	Acres of barley to be tilled	Acres of oats to be tilled
Thomas Hoblyn, gent.	34	10	10	10	10	0
Ralph Keate, gent.	22	30	30	30	10	10
Thomas Lawry	10	30	0	0	0	0
Henry Bligh	14	12	20	10	10	10
James Manhowe	8	10	10	10	5	5
Richard Copithorn	4	20	10	0	8	0
John Roscorlowe	10	10	10	10	10	10
Richard Adaim	6	10	10	16	9	0
Thomas Oxman	6	6	6	6	6	6
John Lawry	10	12	12	12	8	8

Sum total of wheat 154 bushels, of barley 118 bushels, of oats 104 bushels.5

(571) *Petherickpva* [Little Petherick] *parish*

	Persons	Bushels of wheat	Bushels of barley	Bushels of oats	Acres of barley to be tilled	Acres of oats to be tilled
John Stribbly	20	60	60	0	0	0

Sum total of wheat 60 bushels, of barley 60 bushels.

[Total Summary]

Sum total of wheat within the hundred 11000-100-44 bushels.
Sum total of barley within the hundred 11000-200-17 bushels.
Sum total of both 22000-300-61 bushels.
Sum total of oats 1000-900-19 bushels.

Corn sold out of market *Petherickpva* [Little Petherick]
Corn sold
Digory Arter hath sold to John French of *Padestowe* wheat 34 bushels, price 10s the bushel.
Malsters, bakers, brewers, tipplers none.

St *Collomb* [Columb] Major
Corn sold
James Trebell hath bought 5 acres of wheat of Hugh Lawry, price 50s the ['bushel' crossed through] acre.
Thomas Brabyn hath bought of Hugh Lawry 5 acres of wheat, price 50s the acre.
John Dyer hath bought 5 acres of wheat of John Brabyn, price 50s the acre.
Malsters
William Beaford malteth weekly of barley 8 bushels.
Hugh Lawry malteth weekly of barley 8 bushels.
Anthony Whitford malteth weekly of barley 4 bushels.
Thomas Symon malteth weekly of barley 4 bushels.
Bakers
John Adam baketh weekly of wheat 4 bushels.

(57m)

John Dyer baketh weekly of wheat 4 bushels.
Luke Pollord baketh weekly of wheat 3 bushels.
Thomas Skynner baketh weekly of wheat 4 bushels.
William Callaway baketh weekly of wheat 3 bushels.
Tipplers
James Trebell breweth weekly of barley malt 3 bushels.
William Daucaster breweth weekly of barley malt 3 bushels.
Hugh Lawry breweth weekly of barley malt 3 bushels.
Henry Dyer breweth weekly of barley malt 2 bushels.
John Heycraft breweth weekly of barley malt 2 bushels.
John Rice breweth weekly of barley malt 2 bushels.
Anthony Whitfor breweth weekly of barley malt 2 bushels.
Thomas Lawe breweth weekly of barley malt 1 bushel.
Robert Pollard breweth weekly of barley malt 1 bushel.

St Ervan

Corn sold
John Coad, clerk, sold to Pollodor Juell of *Padestowe* of oats 40 bushels.
Tipplers
John Veale breweth weekly of barley malt one bushel.
Malsters & bakers none within the parish.

St *Evall* [Eval]

Corn sellers
Robert Arthur hath sold to John Adam of St *Collomb* Major of wheat twenty bushels, price £8 13s 4d, more sold by him to Hugh Lawry of St *Collomb* Major twenty bushels of barley, price - £7 10s.
Tipplers
Stephen Carthewe breweth weekly of barley malt one bushel.
Ralph Michell breweth once in [a] fortnight one bushel of barley malt.

Lanhidrocke [Lanhydrock]

Bakers
John Goodman baketh weekly of wheat two bushels ['of' crossed through].
Tipplers
William Carhoewe breweth weekly of barley malt one bushel.
Henry Bone breweth once in [a] fortnight one bushel of barley malt.
Malsters none, regraters of corn none.

(57n) *Withiell* **[Withiel]**
Bakers
John Renorden baketh weekly of wheat one half a bushel.
Katherine Mawpowder baketh weekly one half a bushel of wheat.
Mark Gyddly breweth weekly one half a bushel of barley malt.
Malsters none, engrossers none, forestallers none.

St Agnes
Corn sold
John Cleather hath sold twenty bushels of wheat to Mr Edward Cooke of St Allen price £9 10s.
Tipplers
Leonard Tregree breweth weekly of barley malt half a bushel.
John Trevery breweth weekly of barley malt half a bushel.
Richard Daniell breweth weekly of barley malt half a bushel.
Bakers
Thomas Tonkyn baketh weekly of wheat one bushel.
Malsters, regraters, engrossers none.

St Wenn
Tipplers
Hannibal Dunn breweth weekly of barley malt half a bushel.
Petherick Williams breweth weekly of barley malt half a bushel.
Humphrey William breweth weekly of barley malt half a bushel
and baketh of wheat half a bushel.
Malsters, engrossers, forestallers none.

Mawgan [in-Pydar]
Corn sold
Rosecleere Asscott hath sold to William Harris of *Bristowe* [Bristol], merchant, 50 bushels of wheat price £25.
Edward Tregemmowe hath sold to Mr George Beare of St Ervan 40 bushels of wheat, price £20.
Gilbert Caser hath sold to John Dyer of St *Collumb* Major 20 bushels of wheat, price £11.
Oates George hath sold to Thomas Symon of St *Collomb* Minor 20 bushels of barley, price £6.
James Bennett hath sold to Digory Rowe of St Issey 10 bushels of oats, price 30s.
more sold to Mr Gilbert Bligh of St Issey 20 bushels of oats, price £3.
more sold to Edward Daucaster of St *Collomb* Minor 20 bushels of oats, price £3.

(57o)

Robert Jllary hath bought of Thomas Lawry of St *Collomb* Major of wheat & barley 28 acres, price per acre 46s.

The said Jllary hath sold of wheat to Richard Lukas of *Padestowe* 20 bushels, price £7 6s 8d.

more sold by the said Jllary to the said Lukas of wheat 40, bushels price £15 16s,

more sold by the said Jllary to ['the said' crossed through] Thomas Lawry of St *Collomb* Major 40 bushels, price £15.

Malster, engrossers, forestallers - none.

Bakers

Ralph Williams baketh weekly of wheat half a bushel.

Richard Bennett baketh weekly half a bushel of wheat.

Tipplers

Richard Powell breweth weekly one bushel of barley malt.

William Hawke breweth weekly of barley malt one bushel.

Lanivett **[Lanivet]**

Tipplers

John Hicks breweth weekly of barley malt one bushel.

Bakers

David Bennett baketh weekly of wheat 2 bushels.

John Rowe baketh weekly of wheat one bushel.

Perran in Zabulo **[Perranzabuloe]**

Corn sold

Mrs Vesula Colmer, widow, hath sold unto Richard Hill, *Trurowe* [Truro] merchant, 20 bushels of wheat, price 9s per bushel.

John Hocken hath sold unto the foresaid Hill 40 bushels of wheat, price 9s per bushel.

More sold by the said Hockyn to the said Hill 60 bushels of barley, price 6s 8d per bushel.

Thomas Resugga hath sold unto the foresaid Hill 20 bushels of wheat, price 9s per bushel.

John Jenking hath sold unto the foresaid Hill 5 bushels of wheat, price 8s 6d per bushel.

Christopher Cardoll hath sold unto the foresaid Hill 10 bushels of wheat, price 9s per bushel.

Richard Cunny hath sold all his corn in his mowhay unto George Cosgaren of St Allen, price £16.

Bakers

Thomas Williams baketh weekly of wheat two bushels.

(57p)   Perranzabuloe cont'd

Tipplers

Edward Symons breweth weekly of barley malt one bushel.

Richard Williams breweth weekly of barley malt one bushel.

Malsters, engrossers, forestallers - none.

Ennodor [St Enoder]

Corn sold

Joseph Jolly hath sold to Mr Michell of *Trewrowe* 30 bushels of wheat, price 11s per bushel.

William Trevethacke hath sold to one Avery of *Trurowe* 20 bushels of wheat, price £10.

Richard Carveigh of St *Collomb* Major hath sold unto Richard John of *Enodor* so much corn in the mowe as comes to the value of twenty-six pounds.

Bakers, brewers, tipplers, malsters, engrossers, forestallers - none.

Crantocke [Crantock]

Corn sold

Mr Lovis hath sold to Mr Hill of *Trurowe* twenty bushels of wheat, price £9.

More sold by the said Lovis to the foresaid Hill forty bushels of barley, price £6 10s.

Robert Clemowe hath sold to the said Mr Hill forty bushels of wheat, price £18.

Leonard Browne hath sold to the said Mr Hill twenty bushels of wheat, price £9.

More sold by the said Browne to the foresaid Hill twenty bushels of barley, price £5 6s 8d.

Mr Bligh hath sold to John Stephens of *Trurowe* twenty bushels of wheat, price £8 10s.

More sold by the said Bligh to one Skynner twenty bushels of wheat, price £10.

Digory Vivian hath sold to David Lawrence twenty bushels of wheat, price £11.

Thomas Symons hath sold to William Gibbs twenty bushels of wheat, price £9.

Tipplers

William Langston breweth of barley malt weekly one bushel.

Nicholas Eare breweth of barley malt weekly one bushel.

William Sparke breweth of barley malt weekly one bushel.

Malsters, bakers, engrossers, forestallers - none.

Cubart [Cubert]

Corn sold since harvest

Mr Davyes hath sold to Mr Hill of *Truraw* ten bushels of wheat, price 9s per bushel.

John Griggor hath sold to the said Hill twenty bushels of wheat, price 9s per

(57q)
bushel.

Sampson Treglenicke hath sold to John Jenking ten bushels of wheat, price 9s per bushel.

John Hodg hath sold to the said Jenking ten bushels of wheat, price 8s 6d per bushel.

Tipplers

Thomas Jllary breweth weekly of barley malt one bushel.

Malsters, bakers, engrossers, forestallers - none.

Newland [Newlyn East]

Corn sold since harvest

William Gybbs hath sold to Richard Hill of *Trurowe* twenty bushels of wheat £9.

Malsters, tipplers, engrossers, forestallers - none.

[St] Merryn

Corn sold since harvest none.

Malsters, brewers, bakers, tipplers, engrossers, forestallers - none.

St *Breocke* [Breock]

Corn sold

John Prideaux esq. hath sold unto Abraham Jennens of *Saltashe* [Saltash] 40 bushels of wheat, price 10s per bushel.

Nicholas Tredenicke, gent., hath sold unto Abraham Jennins of *Saltashe* 13 bushels of wheat, price 10s per bushel.

Dorothy Wilton, widow, hath sold unto Peane of *Bristowe* 20 bushels of wheat, price 8s the bushel.

More, she the said Dorothy Wilton, hath sold unto some of *Padestowe* 20 bushels of wheat, price 10s the bushel.

Nicholas Dandy hath sold unto the same Peane of *Bristowe* 10 bushels of wheat, price 8s per bushel.

Pennaliggan Richard & William Lukes hath sold unto Abraham Jennins of *Saltashe* 20 bushels of wheat, price 10s per bushel.

Sampson Biscows hath sold unto the foresaid Abraham Jennins 10 bushels of wheat, price 10 per bushel.

Maltmakers

John Hocker sells weekly of barley malt two bushels.

Christopher Francke, junior, sells weekly of barley malt two bushels.

Bakers

Philip Eare baketh of wheat weekly one bushel.

Clement Symens baketh of wheat weekly one bushel.

(57r)   Breocke cont'd

Tipplers

Barcott Pettygrewe breweth weekly of barly malt two bushels.

Samuel Harvey breweth weekly of barley malt two bushels.

William Dandy breweth weekly of barley malt one bushel.

Engrossers and forestallers - none.

St Issey

Corn sold since harvest

Martin Tom hath sold to Abraham Jennins of *Saltashe* twenty bushels of whea,t price £10.

Richard Wills hath sold to Warne Swymner of *Pastowe* ten bushels of wheat, price £5.

William Sandowe hath sold to Abraham Jennins of *Saltashe* six bushels of wheat, price £3.

Digory Udy hath sold to Abraham Jennins of *Saltashe* twenty bushels of wheat, price £10.

More the said Deggory hath sold to William Jolly & Warne Swyner of *Padestowe* 20 bushels of wheat, price £10.

Gilbert Bligh hath sold to Abraham Jennins of *Saltashe* 40 bushels of wheat, price £40.

More the said Gilbert hath sold on the ground to Richard Lucas & Edmund Land of *Padestowe* one hundred & twenty bushels of wheat.

More the said Bligh hath sold unto the said Lucas and Land on the ground of barley 60 bushels.

Dorothy Cornishe, widow, hath sold of wheat on the ground unto John French of *Padestow* 20 acres, price £10 ['£6' crossed through].

John Morcomb hath sold to Arthur Stribbly of Little Petherick 20 bushels of wheat, price £9.

John Bettye hath sold on the ground to Edmund Land & Richard Lucas of *Padestowe* of wheat - 70 bushels.

More sold by the said Betty to the foresaid Land & Lucas of barley, on the ground - 80 bushels.

Nicholas Warne hath sold to Abraham Jennins of *Saltashe* 20 bushels of wheat, price £10.

John Arthur hath sold to William Harris of *Briestowe* of wheat 20 bushels, price £10.

Digory Arter hath sold to Abraham Jennins of *Saltashe* 20 bushels, of wheat price £10.

More sold by the said Degory to William Harris of *Bristowe* 20 bushels, of wheat price £7 10s.

John Prynn hath sold to Abraham Jennins of *Saltashe* 30 bushels of wheat, price £15.

(57s)
Tipplers
John Harris breweth weekly of barley malt one bushel.
John Layty breweth weekly of barley malt one bushel.
Malsters, bakers, brewers, engrossers & forestallers none.

Collomb [St Columb] minor
Corn sold since harvest
Thomas Mundy, gent., hath sold to Richard Hill of *Trurowe* 40 bushels of wheat, price 9s per bushel.
More the said Thomas Mundy hath sold of barley to William Beaford of St *Colom* Major 200 bushels, price 6s 10d per bushel.
John Mundy hath sold to Richard Hill of *Trurowe* 50 bushels of wheat, price 8s 6d per bushel.
More sold to the said Hill twenty bushels, of barley price 6s per bushel.
John Watts hath sold to Richard Hill of *Trurowe* 20 bushels of wheat, price 9s per bushel.
More sold by the said Watts to Mr Lovis ten bushels of wheat, price 9s per bushel.
John Symon hath sold to his neighbours 40 bushels, of wheat for seed price 9s per bushel.
Robert Carne hath sold unto Mr Hill of *Trurowe* 20 bushels of wheat, 9s per bushel.
Henry Cooke hath sold to Mr Hill of *Trurowe* 20 bushels of wheat, price 9s per bushel.
More sold by the said Cooke to John Stephens 20 bushels of wheat, price 9s per bushel.
More sold by the said Cooke to William Bate of *Lassant* [Lezant] 20 bushels of wheat, price 10s per bushel.
Robert Jllary hath sold to Mr Hill of *Trurowe* 10 bushels of wheat, price 10s per bushel.
William Wats hath sold to Hugh Lawry of St *Collomb* Major 10 bushels of barley, price 7s 6d per bushel.
John Sammen hath sold to Hugh Lawry of St *Collomb* Major 20 bushels of barley, price 6s per bushel.
More sold by the said Sammon to Anthony Whitford of St *Collomb* Major 20 bushels of barley, price 6s per bushel.
John Robert jun. hath sold to Mr Hill of *Trurowe* 20 bushels wheat, price 9s per bushel.
More sold by the said Roberts to Richard Boundy 20 bushels of barley, price 6s 8d per bushel.
William Symon sold to Mr Hill of *Trurowe* 10 bushels of wheat, price 9s per bushel.

(57t)   St Columb cont'd

More sold by the said Symon to Hugh Lawry of St *Collomb* 12 bushels of barley, price 6s per bushel.

Richard Stone hath sold to Hugh Lawry of St *Collomb* Major 40 bushels of barley, price 6s 6d per bushel.

['Maltmakers' crossed through]

Leonard Budlye hath sold unto Hugh Lawry of St *Collomb* Major 28 bushels of barley, price 6s 6d per bushel.

John Roberts sen. hath sold unto Anthonly Whitford of St *Collombmajor* 12 bushels of barley, price 6s per bushel.

John Oxanbery hath sold to John Mundye 8 acres wheat in the ground, price 33s 4d per acre.

Maltmakers

Richard Bondye makes weekly of barley malt two bushels.

John Gommowe makes weekly of barley malt one bushel.

Tipplers

John Cane breweth weekly of barley malt one bushel.

Robert Gommowe breweth weekly of barley malt one bushel.

Robert Wise breweth weekly of barley malt one bushel.

Thomas Kestell breweth weekly of barley malt one bushel.

Nicholas Warring breweth weekly of barley malt one bushel.

Bakers

John Stribbly baketh of wheat weekly two bushels.

John Jenkinge baketh of wheat weekly two bushels.

John Stephens baketh of wheat weekly two bushels.

Badgers, engrossers and forestallers none.

Padestowe

Corn sold since harvest

Nyott Doubt hath sold of wheat sixteen bushels, price 8s per bushel.

John Tom hath sold to Abraham Jennins of *Saltashe* 26 bushels of wheat, price 10s per bushel.

Gregory Stribbly hath sold 40 bushels of wheat to Mr Way who is bound for New England, price twenty pounds.

More sold by the said Stribbly to George Short of *Bediford* [Bideford], merchant, 20 bushels of wheat, price £10.

John French hath sold to Mr Way & Mr Jennins of *Saltashe* 30 bushels of wheat, price 11s per bushel.

Jane Blake, widow, hath sold twenty bushels of barley, price £6.

John Warne hath sold twenty bushels of barley, price 6s 6d per bushel.

John Martyn hath sold fourteen bushels of barley, price 6s 8d per bushel.

Peter Petherock hath sold eight bushels of barley, price 6s 8d per bushel.

John Arthur hath sold forty bushels of barley, price 6s 8d per bushel.

Thomas Arthur hath sold ten bushels of wheat, price 11s per bushel.

(57u)

Stephen Parking hath sold twenty bushels of barley, price 6s 8d per bushel.

Malsters

John Prideaux, gent., hath in malt 60 bushels.

More barley to be made into malt 20 bushels.

Ann Ellynworth, widow, hath in malt 20 bushels.

Pollodor Juell hath in malt 100 bushels.

Bakers

Jane Blake, widow, baketh of wheat weekly one bushel.

James Bennett baketh weekly of wheat two bushels.

Maximilian Blake baketh weekly of wheat 3 bushels.

Robert Richards baketh weekly of wheat 2 bushels.

John Fostare baketh weekly of wheat 2 bushels.

Tipplers

Nyott Doubt breweth weekly of barley malt 2 bushels and hath in malt 6 bushels.

Vesula Smyth breweth weekly of barley malt 2 bushels.

John Tom breweth weekly of barley malt one bushel.

John Norman breweth weekly of barley malt one bushel.

Robert Billinge breweth weekly of barley malt 4 bushels.

William Marke breweth weekly of barley malt 4 bushels.

Emmanuel Bruton breweth weekly 3 bushels of barley malt.

John Pears breweth weekly 3 bushels of barley malt.

John Juell breweth weekly 3 bushels of barley malt.

John Jeffry breweth weekly of barley malt 2 bushels.

Marian Quint, widow, breweth weekly of barley malt 2 bushels.

Maximilian Blake breweth weekly of barley malt one bushel.

Warne Swymmer breweth weekly of barley malt 3 bushels.

Badgers, engrossers & forestallers none.

[signed] John Prideaux   Edward Coswarth

58. Certificate. Sir John Roe to the Privy Council, 11 December 1630.

PRO, SP16/176/57

[endorsed. To the Right Honourable the Lords of His Majesty's most honourable Privy Council present these.
11th of December 1630. From Sir John Roe, late Sheriff of the county of Cornwall about the prices of corn there, in answer to one from the Board.]

Right Honourable,

May it please your Lordships to be advertised that whereas about the 20th of

October last I received his Majesty's proclamations and Books of Orders for the preventing of the dearth of grain and victual which being published and the directions therein prosecuted, both by myself and the Justices of the Peace accordingly. Yet the said Justices have not certified me whereby I might particularly certify your Lordships according to the direction of the said orders, the reason as I conceive is because I, being out of office within one month after the receipt of the foresaid proclamations and orders, the said Justices have already or do forthwith intend to certify the now Sheriff. Nevertheless in discharge of my duty and service in this behalf and for answer unto the particulars of a letter which I have received from your Lordships dated at Whitehall the 11th of November last, I do hereby certify your honours that by reason of the due respect had by the Justices to the Orders aforesaid the markets have been plentifully furnished with corn and victual and the transporting and exporting of corn by sea and the buying thereof at men's houses out of the markets which hath been heretofore usual is carefully reformed and yet the price of corn doth still increase, the cause proceeding from the report of the scarcity of corn in some parts of this kingdom and not for any want in this county, there being sufficient for provision for the same both by land and for setting forth our shipping by sea, as hath been heretofore used. And as touching the several prices of corn as it is now sold in the market, wheat is at nine pence half penny the gallon, barley at five pence half penny the gallon, oats at two pence half penny the gallon, I rate it by the gallon because the measure of the bushel in this county is uncertain and this county is not furnished with any other grain besides those three grains aforesaid, I have delivered unto Sir John Trelawny knight and baronet, my successor, the letter before mentioned which I received from your Lordships to prosecute the effect thereof, and thus I humbly take my leave and rest, at your Lordships' service,
[signed] John Roe, late sheriff of Cornwall

from *Bodmyn* in Cornwall, the 11th of December 1630

59. Certificate. Mayor of Dartmouth to the High Sheriff of Devon, 1 February 1631.

PRO, SP16/184/2
[endorsed. To the right worshipful Henry Ashfoord esq. high Sheriff of the county of Devon deliver these.]

Right Worshipful,
It may please you to be advertised that since our last certificate sent unto you in obedience unto his Majesty's royal command we have not again caused the barns within the parish of *Tonnstall* and Dartmouth to be viewed for that there

hath not been any want of corn in our market yet we have thought good hereby to certify that during all the month of December last in our market the usual prices of wheat were 8s 6d, of barley 6s, of malt 7s and of peas 7s and that in the beginning of January last the price of wheat was 9s, of barley 6s 4d, of malt 7s 6d and of peas 7s 6d and that the last week and market day the price of wheat was 9s 6d, of barley 6s 8d, of malt 8s and of peas 8s and that perceiving the prices of grain to increase we have restrained Thomas Abraham from making so great a quantity of malt as he was formerly accustomed and have suppressed divers alehouses within our town and have done our best endeavour to compel the brewers to brew their beer according to the statute and thus being always ready to put his Majesty's commands in execution we take our leave. Dartmouth this first of February 1630 [1631].

Your loving friends,

[signed] Robert Follett, Mayor   John Richards

60. Certificate. High Sheriff of Cornwall to the Privy Council, 5 February 1631.

PRO, SP16/184/16
[endorsed. To the right Honourable the Lords of his Majesty's most honourable Privy Council be these delivered.
for March 1631 Cornwall. from John Trelawny about the prices of corn in the county.]

May it please your Honours to be advertised that whereas heretofore his Majesty's proclamations & Books of Orders have been published in this county of *Cornewall* for the preventing of the dearth of grain & victual, and whereas your honours have been since pleased to direct your letters to my predecessor the late Sheriff, thereby signifying unto him your expectations of an account in the premises both from himself and from me. Albeit, I have not as yet received any certificate from the Justices of the Peace whereby I might particularly certify your honours according to the direction of the said orders. Nevertheless in discharge of my duty and service in this behalf, and in answer to the particulars of the said letter I do hereby certify your Lordships that the Justices of Peace have taken care to see the markets well furnished with corn and to prevent the inconveniences mentioned in the Books of Orders, this county being now as well stored with corn as in any former years it that been, and yet the price is at a higher rate which I conceive rather proceedeth from the report of the scarcity of corn in other parts of this kingdom then for any want in this county. And as for the several prices of corn as it is now sold in the markets within the said county, wheat is at nine pence the gallon, barley at five pence the gallon and oats at two pence half penny the gallon. In regard the measure of the bushel in the said markets is uncertain, I rate it by the gallon. This county

is not stored with any other kind of grain then the several grains before mentioned. And thus with tender of my humble service in this behalf as in all other your honours' commands I rest, at your Lordships' service
[signed] John Trelawny

Launceston this fifth of February 1630 [1631]

61. Certificate. Justices of Plympton, Ermington, Roborough, Tavistock and Lifton hundreds to the High Sheriff of Devon, 10 February 1631.

PRO, SP16/184/60

Mr Sheriff,
Since the time of our late certificate unto this present, we find that the price of corn hath varied very little from what it was at that time and the markets are indifferently well served through out all the several hundreds of Plympton, Ermington, Roborough, *Tavistocke* and Lifton. Witness our hands at *Tavistocke* the tenth day of February 1630 [1631]
[signed] Francis Drake William Strode Edmund Fowell Shilston Calmady Francis Glanvill Sampson Hele Alexander Maynard

62. Certificate. Mayor of Dartmouth to the High Sheriff of Devon, 3 March 1631.

PRO, SP16/186/22
[endorsed. To the right Worshipful and our worthy friend Henry Ashfoord esq. high sheriff of the county of Devon, deliver these.
April 1631 from Devon touching corn.]

Right Wo:,
It may please you to be advertised that in obedience to his Majesty's Royal command we have thought it our duty to certify you that in our market we have observed that during the last month of February there was rather an overplus then any want of any kind of grain, yet wheat was sold the three first market days for 9s and some for 9s 3d, barley for 6s and some for 6s 2d and malt for 7s and some for 8s 6d the bushel, the measure being a bushel and half of the barley measure and the last market day wheat was sold for 9s 6d and some for 9s 9d, barley for 6s 4d and some for 6s 2d, malt for 9s and peas for 8s the bushel and we have done the utter most of our endeavour to hinder the brewing of

strong beers and strong ale and do license no more tipplers or alehouse-keepers within our town then are convenient for the town being a port town and much resorted unto be strangers. We have also taken recognizances of all innholders, vintners, alehousekeepers within our town for the due keeping of Lent and observing of the fish days and fasting days commanded by the law throughout the year, and do as much as in us punish all alehouse haunters and other disordered persons and will not slack in the due execution of his Majesty's commands.

And will rest, your very loving friends

[signed] Robert Follett, Mayor   John Richards

Dartmouth this 3rd of March 1630 [1631]

63. Certificate. Mayor of Dartmouth to the High Sheriff of Devon, 4 April 1631.

PRO, SP16/188/15
[endorsed. 4 April 1632. To the right worshipful Henry Ashfoord esq. High Sheriff of the county of Devon deliver these.]

Right Worshipful,

In obedience unto his Majesty's command I have thought it my duty to certify you, that our market during all the last month was insufficiently supplied with all sorts of grain so that there was no want, and that during the three first market days wheat was sold for nine shillings and six pence the bushel, barley for six shillings and four pence the bushel, and malt for eight shillings and six pence the bushel but the last market day wheat was sold for ten shillings, malt for nine shillings and barley for six shillings and eight pence the bushel. And also that within our liberties I have done the uttermost of my endeavour to suppress all unnecessary alehouses and to constrain those which are licensed to brew and sell according to the law in that case made and provided, wherein as in all other things I shall ever be ready and willing to manifest my obedience and discharge my duty. And will always rest, your very loving friend,

[signed] Robert Follett, Mayor

Dartmouth this 4th of April 1631

64. Certificate. Justices of Axminster, Colyton, East Budleigh, Ottery St Mary and Cliston hundreds to the High Sheriff of Devon, 21 April 1631.

PRO, SP16/189/5
[endorsed. To the right worshipful Henry Ashfoorde esq. high sheriff of the county of Devon these.
for his Majesty's service.]

Devon
This certificate is for the hundreds of Axminster, Colyton, East *budleighe,* Ottery St Mary and Cliston: the measures 9 and somewhere 10 gallons.

Worthy Sir:
In our last we gave you to understand how the prices of corn then stood in our parts. Since which time by means of the scarcity of corn which as we find our markets daily to rise, wheat being now generally at 12s the bushel and some higher (though our measure be the least of this county. Barley, peas are at 7s ordinarily and some times more. We much doubt it is not yet at the highest, we find also a great complaint among the poor that they can not get corn for money. Our markets being very thinly furnished though we have again issued warrants to supply that defect. We have raised the Book of the poor to as great a proportion as we may so that such as are taxed complain on the other side. In some parishes we have taken views of particular poor families and hath given order for the billeting of divers poor children of such as by their labour are not able to support their charge, others we have placed abroad as apprentices, so that we now know not what may remaineth for us to do more, considering the great burthens of the persons of every quality and deadness of the time. Thus having once again given you account of our doings according to the orders prescribed we rest, your loving friends
[signed] Peter Prideaux   John Pole   Walter Yonge   Nicholas Fry

21rst April 1631

65. Certificate. High Sheriff of Cornwall to the Privy Council, 1 May 1631.

PRO, SP16/190/2
[endorsed. To the right honourable the Lords of his Majesty's Privy Council present these.
Conewall. 18 of May 1631 from the High sheriff of *Cornewall* about the prices of corn.]

May it please your honours to be advertised that since my last letter to your honours dated the tenth day of February last I have received these enclosed certificates from the Justices of the Peace of this county of *Cornwall* touching corn. And I do further certify your Lordships that the price of corn is now of late abated, so that wheat is now at 7d a gallon, barley at 4d the gallon and oats at 2d the gallon. And thus with the tender of my humble service in this behalf I rest, at your Honours' Command

[signed] John Trelawny

Dated 1 May 1631

66. Certificate. Justices of Lensnewth hundred to the High Sheriff of Cornwall, 20 April 1631.

PRO, SP16/190/2(i)
[endorsed. To the right wo: our good friend Sir John Trelawny knight and baronet high sheriff of the county of *Cornewall.*
April the 20th 1631. Monaton knight, Tristram Arscott Justices Cornwall.]

Good Sir,
Shortly after the receipt of the Book of Orders and directions from you, granted by his Majesty, we appointed our last quarter sessions to be held at *Camelfourd* [Camelford] for the hundred of *Lesnewthe* the 13th day of this instant where (as formerly we were moved to do) we bound out about sixteen apprentices to be brought up in husbandry and then gave directions and charges to the overseers for the poor of the several parishes respectively within that hundred for the placing abroad of all such poor children within their parishes as were or are fit to be bound out as apprentices and we have thought good to let you know that at the foresaid meeting we then proceeded with negligent comers to the church, swearers, drunkards, alehouse haunters and unlicensed alehouse keepers (by inflicting the penalties of the laws upon the offenders according to their several demerits) upon such as we found guilty in that behalf and so our best respects to you remembered we rest your very loving friends,
[signed] Ambrose Monaton esq. Tristram Arscott

20 April 1631

67. Certificate. Justices of part of East hundred to the High Sheriff of Cornwall, 20 April 1631.

PRO, SP16/190/2(ii)
[endorsed. To the right wo: Sir John Trelawny knight and baronet high Sheriff of the county of *Cornewall* these deliver.
Cornwall April the 20th 1631. William Corlton & Monaton Justices.]

Good Mr Sheriff,
These are to give you knowledge that shortly after receipt of the Book of Orders and directions from you granted by the King's Majesty we appointed a meeting at *Kellyton* [Callington] the 15th day of April 1631 (the place most convenient for the work from part of the hundred of East and within the limit of our division where we bound out thirty apprentices to be brought up in husbandry and then punished the negligent comers to the church on Sundays and holy days, swearers, drunkards and unlicensed alehouse keepers and alehouse haunters by inflicting the full penalties of the law upon the several offenders, to be converted to the use of the poor of each parish respectively where the offence were committed according to the laws which we have thought good to certify you under our hands and so we remain, your very loving friends,
[signed] William Coryton   Ambrose Monaton

20 April 1631

68. Letter. High Sheriff of Cornwall to the Privy Council, 6 May 1631.

PRO, SP16/190/37

May it please your Lordships,
According to the directions from the Lord Commissioners I caused the six Books of Orders and two letters which I received from their Lordships with a copy of their Lordships' letter to be sent and delivered to the Justices of the Peace and Mayors of towns in the several divisions of this county of *Cornewall* since which time I have not received any certificate from any of them of their proceedings therein but only those which herein I present unto your Lordships after tender of my due respect I humbly take my leave and rest, your Lordships' servant,
[signed] John Trelawny

Trelawne 6 May 1631

69. Certificate. Justices of Trigg hundred to the High Sheriff of Cornwall, 28 January 1631.

PRO, SP16/190/37(i)

Cornwall
To the sheriff of the county aforesaid,
This are to certify you that according to his Majesty's proclamation dated the 28th of September last and Orders thereupon we have made enquiry and proceeded according to the tenor of the articles therein mentioned within the hundred of Trigg and we do find that the corn to be sold within the said hundred doth amount to the several number of bushels, following accounting 20 gallons to the bushel, *vizt* in the parish of *Bodmyn* [Bodmin] 20 bushels of barley, in the parish of Blisland 62 bushels of wheat, 49 bushels of barley, 81 bushels of oats, in the parish of St Teath 170 bushels of wheat, 10 bushels of barley, 40 bushels of oats, in the parish of [St] Minver 599 bushels of wheat, 346 bushels of barley, in the parish of St *Tudie* [Tudy] 84 bushels of wheat, 67 bushels of barley, 30 bushels of oats, in the parish of *Endelion* [St Endellion] 349 bushels of wheat, 366 bushels of barley, 60 bushels of oats, in the parish of St *Mabin* [Mabyn] 280 bushels of wheat, 246 bushels of barley, 100 bushels of oats, in the parish of *Egloshaile* [Egloshayle] 320 bushels of wheat, 314 bushels of barley, in the parish of Helland 18 bushels of wheat, 12 bushels of barley, in the parish of [St] Breward 16 bushels of wheat, 10 bushels of barley, 36 bushels of oats, in the parish of St *Kewe* [Kew] 484 bushels of wheat, 100 bushels of barley, 62 bushels of oats and we are informed that the one half of the said corn which is to be sold is not sufficient for the use of such persons within the said hundred as want corn and must buy the same before next harvest and we find that the usual prices of wheat in the markets there adjoining is 13s 6d, the bushel of barley 9s the bushel, of rye 10s the bushel and of oats 4s the bushel.
[signed] John Prideaux Ambrose Manaton esq.
28 January 1630 [1631]

70. Certificate. Justices of Lesnewth hundred to the High Sheriff of Cornwall, 8 January 1631.

PRO, SP16/190/37(ii)

Cornwall
To the Sheriff of the county aforesaid,
This is to certify you that according to his Majesty's proclamation dated the

28th of September last and Orders thereupon we have made enquiry of the articles therein mentioned within the hundred of Lesnewth in the said hundred ['and we find that' crossed through] which doth contain 17 parishes and we do find that the corn to be sold within the said parishes doth amount to the several number of bushels following accounting the wheat and barley to 16 gallons the bushel and the oats to 20 gallons, *vizt* in the parish of Lesnewth 52 bushels of wheat and four bushels of barley, in the parish of St Gennys threescore and six bushels of wheat, one hundred and twenty bushels of oats and ten bushels of barley, in the parish of *Tintagell* [Tintagel] 81 bushels of wheat, 61 bushels of barley, 10 bushels of oats, in the parish of *Dewstoe* [Davidstow] 62 bushels of oats, in the parish of Otterham 14 bushels of wheat, in the parish of *Warpstowe* [Warbstow] 22 bushels of wheat, in the parish of *Trevalgo* [Trevalga] 14 bushels of wheat, 11 bushels of barley and 14 bushels of oats, in the parish of St Clether no corn to be spared or sold, in the parish of Advent none to be sold, in the parish of St *Julet* [Juliot] 26 bushels of wheat and 10 of barley, in the parish of Lanteglos[-by-Camelford] no corn to be spared, in the parish of *Michaelstowe* [Michaelstow] 12 bushels of wheat, in the parish of *Poundstocke* [Poundstock] 37 bushels of wheat, in the parish of *Alternon* [Altarnun] ['of wheat' crossed through] 138 bushels of wheat, 10 bushels of rye, 187 bushels of oats, in the parish of Treneglos 32 bushels of wheat, 78 bushels of oats, in the parishes of Minster and *Forraberie* [Forrabury] no corn to be sold or spared, and we are given to understand by the parishioners of the said parishes that the corn to be sold and spared will not be sufficient to suffice the persons which buy their corn within the said hundred before the next harvest and we do further certify that the usual price of wheat in the markets there adjoining is 11s 6d the bushel, of barley 7s the bushel, of rye 9s the bushel, and of oats 4[s] 4d the bushel.

[signed] John Prideaux Ambrose Monaton esq.

28 January 1630 [1631]

71. Certificate of Justices of part of East hundred, 8 February 1631.

PRO, SP16/190/37(iii)

North Division of the hundred of East. Cornwall.

A certificate of all our doings and proceedings touching the preventing and remedying of the dearth of grain and other victuals in our said division according to his Majesty's Orders in that behalf dated the 28th day of September 1630.

First, we did in December last precept and convent before us a certain number of the most honest and substantial inhabitants in our division and gave them then in charged the articles required by the Book.

That on the 29th day of the same month they brought us in their presentments to every part of the articles in charge from point to point.

We found by those presentments little corn to be spared within our said division (their own families provided for) and the poorer sort of the several parishes supplied.

What we conceived might be spared; gave order that the same should be proportionally brought into the next markets, vizt Launceston and Liskeard, the which we are confident is accordingly done.

We took course that no corn should be bought to be sold again nor no corn to be bought but in open markets.

We did then in a convenient sort, restrain common malsters from making barley malt and endeavoured and still do endeavour to lessen the number of maltmakers, common brewers and tipplers.

We have suppressed all badgers, kiddiers, broggers and carriers of corn (except such as were and are licensed according to the law.

We find no engrossers of corn within our division, nor any transportation of corn, having in our said division neither port, creek, haven or maritime town.

We have given strict charge and commandment that the Assize of bread and beer shall be duly kept and observed, and that such bread as shallbe found faulty to be forthwith sold towards the relief of the poorer.

We have given likewise strict command that no Friday's supper be made in inns, taverns, alehouses or tippling houses & not any waste of bread corn superfluously nor any expense thereof but for the feeding of people.

We have given commandment that no millers be suffered to be common buyers of corn either in markets or out of markets.

We have in our division but one market town which is Launceston, the which is by this means well served with corn and the prices there every market day is rather fallen and abated then increased, wheat being now at 10s the bushel in 16 gallons the bushel, and so hath been for this month last past and was formerly at 12s the bushel & all other manner of grain being fallen in the price proportionally.

The northern division of this hundred of east which is our said division, doth serve ['no' crossed through] the markets with corn, not only Launceston and Saltash but Liskeard also the division containing 21 parishes.

There is no more Justices in this division absent from this service but Mr Coryton who at the time of our sitting and long before was in London about special business and affairs of his own.

These and all other things contained in the printed books we will from time to time see to be observed and pursue the same according to the orders and directions therein given under our hands this 8th day of February 1630 [1631].

[signed] W: Wrey   Ambrose Monaton esq.

72. Certificate of the viewers of the barns in Tiverton,[2] received May 1631.

PRO, SP16/192/95
[endorsed. May 1631. from the Justices of the Peace in the county of Devon about the prices of corn.]

Devon   Tiverton

We the viewers of the barns for Pitt quarter within the parish of Tiverton (whose names are subscribed) do find that there as yet remaineth two hundred bushels of corn which is for the market of Tiverton aforesaid.
[signed] Nicholas Tremlett   Jeffrey Gill   John Kerslake   William Fursey
William Speare

We the viewers of the barns for ['Pitt' crossed through] Tidcombe quarter within the parish of Tiverton (whose names are subscribed) do find that there is yet remaining within the said market two hundred & fifty bushels of corn which is for the market of Tiverton aforesaid.
[signed] John Chamberline   Michael Osmond   John Pasmore   William Crose
Thomas Reade

We the viewers of the barns for Clare quarter within the parish of Tiverton (whose names are subscribed) do find that there is yet remaining within the said quarter one hundred & fifty bushels of corn which is for the market of Tiverton aforesaid.
[signed] John Reede   Robert Pitt   William Land   Roger Webber
William Downe

We the viewers of the barns for Priory quarter within the parish of Tiverton (whose names are subscribed) do find that there is yet remaining within the said quarter twenty bushels of corn, which is for the market of Tiverton aforesaid.
[signed] William Hagley   Richard Rooke   John Ellys   William Squint
Simon Hatswell

73. Certificate. Justices of Ermington, Plympton, Roborough, Tavistock and Lifton hundreds to the High Sheriff of Devon, 4 June 1631.

PRO, SP16/193/25
[endorsed. To the right worshipful Henry Aishford esq. Sheriff of the county of Devon.
June 1631 from Devon touching corn.]

Worthy Sir,

These are in confirmeth to the orders lately received from the Lords of his Majesty's most honourable Privy Council to certify you of the common prices of corn in the several hundreds of Ermington, Plympton, Roborough, *Tavistocke* & Lifton which are as followeth

wheat per bushel - 11s
barley per bushel - 7s
rye per bushel - 9s
oats 3s 6d

Your very loving friends,

[signed] William Strode   Edmund Fowell   Francis Glanvill   Sampson Hele   Alexander Maynard

Plympton 4 June 1631

74. Certificate. Justices of Hayridge, Bampton, Hemyock, Halberton and Tiverton hundreds to the Privy Council, 20 November 1631.

PRO, SP16/203/56
[endorsed. December 1631 from the county of Devon touching corn]

To the right honourable the Lords of his Majesty's most honourable Privy Council.

Most humbly advertiseth your Lordships Sir Thomas Drewe, Sir Symon Leach knight & Henry Walrond esq., his Majesty's Justices of the Peace amongst others in the county of Devon & dwelling in the east division of the said county, that whereas we received your Lordships' letters directed unto the Justices of this county dated the 18th of October last, thereby requiring us within our several divisions by a strict & diligent examination to find our what quantity of corn there was remaining in the said county of the last year's store, hoarded up by any persons & not brought into the market & also by what combination or indirect practice of corn-masters & farmers the prices of corn have been so extremely enhanced in the last year, & are still kept up beyond expectation, we in obedience unto your Lordships' charge in his Majesty's name laid upon us according our bounden duties in that behalf (having used all possible care & diligence in the punctual observation of your Lordships' said letters, by enquiring throughout every particular parish of these five hundreds in the said East division *viz Harridge* [Hayridge], Bampton, *hemyocke* [Hemyock], Halberton & Tiverton being the next hundreds whereunto we are always billeted for services of that nature) can find no combination nor indirect practice to have been used by corn-masters or farmers in the said five hundreds of the said division: but on the contrary we can truly certify unto you Lordships that upon such command & directions as we received from his Majesty out of his most gracious & princely care to have your markets well replenished with corn for the better relief especially of the poorer sort of his subjects before the last harvest we found the said corn-masters & farmers very conformable in bringing forth their corn into the markets & selling of it there according. By his Majesty's said command & directions they were required by us after such good proportion of all sorts of grain as it might hold out to replenish the said markets until the next harvest. And we cannot find by our said enquiry that there was any old corn hoarded up by any man, or that there was any quantity of corn left in any farmer's or corn-master's hands after the end of the last harvest worth the relating unto your Lordships and that the great price of corn did grow with us in the said five hundreds by reason of the scarcity of corn (which was far inferior to the plenty of other years) rather then by any combination or indirect practices of any corn-masters or farmers of these parts. And we must further advertise your Lordships that we have caus[ed] some persons who have regrated some small quantity of corn to the offence of the poor people to be severely punished according to the law. And in point of transportation of corn (although there be no such matter to be doubted of within these five hundreds, being far remote from the sea) we will be very willing to observe your Lordships and in preventing of the same & of observing any other direction in you Lordship's letters contained. And so we most humbly take our leaves,

Your Lordships' in all due obedience to be commanded,
[signed] Thomas Drewe Simon Leache Henry Walrond
dated the 20th of November 1631

75. Certificate. Justices of Haytor, Teingbridge and parts of Exminster and Wonford hundreds to the Privy Council, 23 November 1631.

PRO, SP16/203/64
[endorsed. for his Majesty's especial service. To the right honourable the Lords of his Majesty's most honourable Privy Council present these. George Chudleigh. December 1631 from the county of Devon touching corn.]

May it please your Lordships,
Your Lordships' letters commanding a certificate what stores of old corn were remaining in this county of Devon at harvest and who they are that have withheld it from the market have been dispersed to the subdivisions of this county. The hundreds of Haytor, *Tingbridge*, part of Exminster and Wonford South falling to our examination, we find by the presentments of the petty

constables that the old corn did with some difficulty bring in the new. And that there was little or no corn left in any man's custody within the parts aforesaid after harvest fully ended. That the price of corn hath not been over low since harvest, we conceive the reason to be that the seed time is but lately past. A bushel of wheat in the market of Newton [Abbot] being thirteen gallons is this day sold for seven shillings & six pence the best, and this is the dearest market in the division, so as we hope through the plenty which it pleased God this year to bestow upon the country and the peoples charity we shall have no cause to put his Majesty's last year's instructions in execution. If there be, your Lordships shall find, us very obedient of your present commands and in all things else.

Your Lordship's most humble and obedient servants,
[signed] George Chudleigh Richard Reynell John Upton
November 23rd 1631

76. Certificate. Justices of Coleridge, Stanborough, Ermington and Plympton hundreds to the Privy Council, 24 November 1631.

PRO, SP16/203/67
[endorsed. To the right honourable the Lords of his Majesty's most honourable Privy Council these deliver.
December 1631. from the county of Southampton (sic) touching corn.]

May it please your Lordships,
We whose names are subscribed in obedience to your Lordships letters concerning the examination of the hoarding up of corn into private hands the last year and for the causing of the markets to be well furnished this year do humbly according to your commands certify that we sent forth our warrants into the several hundreds of *Colrudge, Stanborrough*, Ermington & Plympton within the county of Devon requiring the constables to make diligent enquiry and strict examination within their several divisions as well what quantity of corn of the last year's store were remaining at the end of the said year hoarded up by any persons and not brought into the markets according to his Majesty's orders as likewise by what combination and indirect practice of the farmers and corn masters or upon what other cause the prices of corn within their divisions were the last year & yet are held at so high rate who appearing before us did severally certify and present that they had made diligent enquiry and yet could not find any person who had hoarded up corn or transgressed his Majesty's said orders for corn and could not learn of any transportation, combination or practice heretofore or now used to hold up the prices thereof, which presentments we did receive and believing to be true because that both the last year and this instant the markets are well furnished and the prices of corn (God be thanked)

not very high for wheat is usually sold the bushel after Winchester measure 4s 8d, barley 3s, oats 2s 6d and it shall be our duty and care according to our places to see his Majesty's laws and orders to be observed to the comendation of them that do observe them and to take special notice of them which transgress or neglect them for their deserved punishment and so humbly desiring your Lordships to receive us and this our certificate into your Honourable & wanted favour we remain,

Your Lordships in all service to be commanded,

[signed] Edmund Fowell William Cory Sampson Hele

dated 24th November 1631

77. Certificate. Justices of Roborough, Tavistock and Lifton hundreds[3] to the Privy Council, 25 November 1631.

PRO, SP16/203/69

[endorsed. To the right honourable our very good Lords, the Lords of his Majesty's most honourable Privy Council, these deliver.]

May it please your Lordships,

According to the commands which we lately received from your honours for an enquiry to be made what quantities of corn of the last year's store were remaining at the end of the said year hoarded up by any persons and not brought into the markets as likewise by what combination & indirect practice of the farmers & corn masters the prices of corn were raised the last year and are still kept up beyond expectation after a plentiful harvest. We have taken both the speediest and strictest course we could to find out within the hundreds of *Roboroughe, Tavistocke & Lyfton* such as have against the law offended and not withstanding the diligence that hath been used, and care taken, we find not any one man that hath either hoarded up corn of the last year (for many amongst us sold so much as [so that] they had not sufficient to bring in the new harvest) or that combined or practised to raise the price then, or keep it up now, neither can we find any cause why the prices of corn were raised the last year immediately upon the putting in execution of the orders we received, other than an ignorant fear in the common people in general that the scarcity was much greater than indeed it was in these parts as was soon after discovered by the good plenty brought into the markets, whereupon the price was well abated before harvest, albeit these parts can hardly endure one bad year. At this present the prices of corn here are very moderate and cannot be expected much lower at any time especially so long as the tillers thereof have little other means to pay the rent of their grounds and pay dear for all things they must buy for their necessary use as salt and the like, which they can not want. The consideration whereof, as also that one & the same rule doth not always serve for all places

in one & the same county, we humbly submit unto your Lordships' approved
wisdoms & remain, your Lordships' humble servants,
[signed] Francis Drake William Strode Shilston Calmady Francis Glanvill
Alexander Maynard

Tavistocke the 25th of November 1631

78. Certificate. Justices of Witheridge and North Tawton hundreds⁴ to the Privy Council, 27 November 1631.

PRO, SP16/203/83
[endorsed. To the right honourable the Lords of His Majesty's most honourable
Privy Council give these.
Mr Dickensen.
December 1631.
A certificate from [blank] touching corn]

Right Honourable,
According to the contents of your Lordships' letters, we have made diligent
enquiry and taken a strict examination of the country, touching the hoarding
and transportation of corn or combination or indirect practise used ['used'
crossed through] by any farmer or corn-master within our division for the
enhancing, raising or holding up of the price thereof, and find not any[one]
delinquent in that kind: But such as had any corn to spare (since the receipt of
his Majesty's late Book of Orders) have, and do, bring the same to the markets
as by virtue of the said Books) we enjoined and commanded them, and we have
not been any way remiss or negligent in that behalf but have used all care and
diligence in performing our duties therein, do humbly take our leaves.
[signed] Edward Chichester Lewis Pollard John Wood
27 November 1631

79. Certificate. Justices of Stanborough and Coleridge hundreds to the High Sheriff of Devon, n.d.

PRO, SP16/184/3

Good Mr Sheriff,
We here present unto you according to the instructions formerly received from
the Lords of his Majesty's most honourable Privy Council a certificate of the
usual prices of the several sorts of corn sold at Kingsbridge and Dodbrooke
being the market towns in the several hundreds of Stanborough and *Colridge*

which are as they follow, that is to say

wheat about thirteen gallons - 8s
barley about thirteen gallons - 5s 8d
oats eighteen gallons - 4s 4d
rye none or little sold in this market

And withal we further signify that the market is weekly very well furnished with all the said sorts of grain, and for the rest of the directions we shall be careful to our best to see them duly executed and so commending our best services unto you we rest, your loving friends,
[signed] Edmund Fowell William Bastard Sampson Hele Thomas Risdon

80. Certificate. Justices of Haytor, Teignbridge and parts of Wonford, Exminster and Stanborough hundreds to the High Sheriff of Devon, n.d.

PRO, SP16/187/91
[endorsed. To our very loving friend Henry Aishford esq. sheriff of the county of Devon these be delivered.]

Sir,
From this our meeting occassioned by the Book of dirrections lately received through your hands, it is reason we satisfy your desire in giving you the notice that we have dispersed the Books you sent to the subdivisions of this South and that the hundreds allotted to our care (by ancient usage) are Haytor, *Tingbridge,* Wonford South and part of Exminster and *Stanborroughe.* In these we shall endeavour to express the obedience we owe to his Majesty's present commands and hope likewise to manifest that the diligence which could have formerly used in his Majesty's service cannot be much improved by the survey of any eyes besides those of our consciences if a second certificate be ex['pressed ' crossed through]pected concerning the execution of the former orders for corn we can add nothing to the first some corn masters we find and many feeders yet corn bears a tolerable price. A bushel of wheat of 12 gallons being about 9s. We shall be vigilant to moderate it upon occasion and till then we are wary not to raise the price by too much striving to date it. And this we conceive will give satisfaction. It is likewise our desire that we may appear to yourself, your assured friends and servants,
[signed] George Chudleigh Richard Reynell Thomas Clyfford John Upton
Thomas Forde Richard Cabell

81. Certificate. Justices of Crediton, and parts of Exminster and Wonford hundreds to the Privy Council, n.d.

PRO, SP16/203/105
[endorsed. to the right honourable the Lords of his Majesty's most honourable Privy Council present these.
for his Majesty's especial service. Nicholas Martyn]

Right Honourables,
We have received your Lordships' letters concerning the hoarding up of corn and the enhancing the prices thereof according to which we have made diligent enquiry and examination throughout all the parts of our division but can find none that hoarded up any corn the last year or that had any left at the end, thereof more then to serve their own needful use until the end of harvest. But that many who had stacks or mowes of corn did then thresh them out and brought the corn weekly into the markets (as we ordered them upon your Lordships' letters). As for the prices of corn now present, the husbandman affirmeth it is not very high considering the great rate that is upon all other commodities and the charge of manuring his ground which is more than formerly hath been. Since we find the markets well furnished with corn of all sorts and the prices not to exceed six shilling eight pence the bushel of wheat and of rye five [shillings] and of barley three shillings eight pence our measure being ten gallons. We have been jealous of transportation and have therefore made enquiry for such offenders but cannot find any, yet we shall not give over our daily care to prevent any such courses in our divisions and shall be ever ready (as in duty we are bound) to spend the best of our endeavours in observing these and all other your Lordships' commands,
Your Lordships most humble and obedient servants
[signed] Nicholas Martyn John Northcot Richard Waltham
Bartholomew Berrye John Bampfelde John Davie

1. Mohun lived at Hall, Lanteglos and Bastard resided in Duloe parish.
2. It must have been sent between 3 and 29 November 1630: see xxxiv.
3. This was probably to the High Sheriff of Cornwall but possibly direct to the Privy Council.
4. Edward Chichester resided at Eggesford in the parish of that name, Lewes Pollard was of Bishop's Nympton and John Wood was possibly of Brixton.

APPENDIX A

82. Letter. William Carnan to Sir Robert Kiligrew, 7 October 1630.

PRO, SP16/174/14.
[endorsed. To the honourable Sir Robert Killigrewe knight vice-chamberlain to the Queen's Majesty these be delivered at the court.
7 October 1630. A letter to Sir Robert Killigrew]

Honourable,
My duty most humbly remembered. I received at *Exon* of Mr Tickle by your letter at my return from London £70 with which I have made up £125 & have paid the same unto Sir William Killigrewe for his quarteridge due at Michaelmas last.

By what warrant I know not there is at least 10000 bushels of wheat & much upwards taken up & intended to be bought here in the west part of Cornwall by several English merchants, whether meant to be ['transported' crossed through] imported to other places of this realm or transported it is not certainly known, but the merchants give out that it is to be imported to other places within the land, about this place there is 4000 bushels taken up & bought some at 9s, some at 10s the bushel, our bushel is 20 gallons, the best men here for the most part are corn merchants & care not for the high price of corn & therefore do not much stir therein, at my coming hence ['where' crossed through] wheat was sold for 8s the bushel & now by this means in less than three weeks it is risen to 12s & if this corn pass here it will be before Easter next at 20s the bushel, for that this time the markets are not served & the bakers have not any place left where they may provide themselves, If the markets be unfurnished the poor & such as till no corn which are commonly people that dwell in towns and till no corn will want & some perish. I write hereof because perhaps there may be petition made to his Majesty or to the Lord Treasurer herein which if there be your honour may safely (if you think good) affirm this for truth. In this grievance many will have a share & my self one. I humbly refer all to the grave consideration of such as may redress it & for my boldness herein do submit myself and do most humbly remain, your honours's most humble servant,
[signed] William Carnan   Penryn this 7th of October 1630.

APPENDIX B

83. The Book of Orders on dearth, 1 June 1608.
Short Title Catalogue 9217.

Orders appointed by his Majesty to be straightly observed for the preventing and remedying of the dearth of grain and other victual.
Dated the first day of June 1608.

That the Sheriff and Justices of the Peace shall immediately upon the receipt of these Orders, assemble themselves together with as much speed as they possible may: And having conferred amongst themselves upon the Contents hereof shall first for the better execution of the same, divide themselves into sundry companies, and take amongst them into their charge, by several divisions, all the Hundreds, Rapes or Wapentakes of the said county.

Item, Every company so allotted out, shall forthwith direct their Precepts unto the High Constables, that they shall cause the Under Constables and other the most honest and substantial Inhabitants within the same Hundred, Rape, or Wapentake to the number of 36 persons, more or fewer, as the quantity of the Hundred, Rape or Wapentake shall require, to appear before them at a certain place and within as short time after the receipt hereof as they conveniently may, and upon the appearance of the said persons, they shall divide them into so many Numbers or Companies as they shall think meet, giving instructions to the said High Constables to return as few of such as be known great farmers for Corn, or that have store of Grain to sell, as he can. And such of the persons so warned as shall not appear, but make default being summoned, and not having any just or reasonable excuse allowable by the Justices, to be punished therefore at the good discretions of the Justices, before whom they are to appear.

Item, they shall first declare to the parties appearing, the cause why they are sent for, and therewith earnestly charge them in the fear of God, to apply themselves to the service where unto they shall be now called, with all dutifulness and diligence, and without any partiality to any person: and then shall give them the charge following:

The Charge

You shall diligently and carefully enquire, and make true and due search and trial, what number of persons of every householder that hath Corn in their Barns, Stacks, or other where, as well Justices of the Peace as others whatsoever, within the Parish of [blank] have in their houses feeding, lying and uprising, or otherwise to be fed: what numbers of Acres they have certainly to be sown this year with any manner of Grain: what bargains they have made with any person for any kind of Grain to be sold, by, or to them: to whom and by whom, and upon what prices they have made the same, and what quantity of any manner of Grain, they, or any other have in their Barns, Granaries, Lofts, Cellars, or Floors, or otherwise to be delivered unto them upon any Bargain.

Item, what number of Badgers, Kiddiers, Broggers or Carriers of Corn inhabit within the said Parish, and whether they do use to carry their Corn which they do buy, and where they do usually buy the same, and what their names be, and how long they have used that trade, and by whose licence, and to see the same licenses of what tenor they are of.

Item, what number of malt makers, bakers, common brewers or tipplers dwell within the said parish, and who they are by name and how long they have used that trade and how much they bake or brew in the week, and what other trade they have whereby otherwise to live.

Item, who within the said parish be the buyers of corn, or do use to buy, or have bought any corn or grain to sell again or have sold it again since the feast of the Annunciation last past.

Item who within the same parish buyeth or have bought or sold any grain upon the ground, of whom, and to whom hath the same been bought or sold, and at what price, and to certify unto us of the premises, and of every part thereof on the [blank] day of [blank] now next coming: and to every part of these articles you shall bring answer from point to point.

And if any shall refuse to declare the truth, of, or concerning the premises, or of any part thereof, to any of the Inquirers aforesaid, requiring the same for their better information: the party so required and refusing, shallbe convented before the Justices of the Peace of the said division, or any two of them, and sharply rebuked, or if need be, punished for his contempt. And if the party so called in question, shall not declare the full truth thereof to the said justices, he shall be committed by the said justices to the common gaol, as a person bound for his good behaviour, and so to be continued, until he shall conform himself therein, or otherwise at the discretions of the said justices, he shall be bound in a good sum of money to make appearance before the Lords of his Majesty's Privy Council to answer unto his contempt in that behalf, for example of all such disobedient persons.

That the said Justices of the Peace having received into their hands the presentment of the said Inquirers answering to every point of their charge, shall call at certain days by them to be assigned, such persons before them of every parish, as upon the presentment so made shall appear to have corn to spare, and upon due consideration of the number of persons, which every person hath in his house, according to their qualities, and of the quantity of grain, that the party hath toward the finding of the same, or otherwise to be spent in his house and sowing of his grounds, allowing to every householder for his expenses in his house, for every person according to their quality, sufficient corn for bread and drink between this and the next harvest, and for their seed after the rate of the sowing of that country upon an acre. And then they shall charge all such as shall appear to have more of any kind of grain, then shall serve to the uses above-mentioned, aswell Justices of the Peace as others to observe the orders ensuing, *viz.*

The orders to be observed are these, *viz.*

You shall bring or cause to be brought weekly so many quarters or bushels of corn, as wheat, rye, barley, malt, peason, beans, or other grain, or so much thereof as shall not be directly sold to the poor artificers or day labourers of the parish within which you dwell, by order of the Justices of the Peace of the division within which you dwell, or two of them, to the market of [blank] there to be by you, or at your assignment sold unto the King's subjects in open market by half quarters, two bushels, one bushel or less, as the buyer shall require of you, and not in greater quantity, except it be to a badger or carrier of corn admitted according to the statute, or to a common known brewer or baker, having testimony under the hand and seal of such two Justices of the Peace at the least of the division, or of a Mayor or other head officer of the city, town or borough corporate where he dwelleth, that he is common brewer or baker within the same: or to such other person as shall make provision for any lord spiritual or temporal, knight, or any other gentleman that hath no sufficient provision of corn, so as the same person have and show unto such persons as shall have the oversight of the market in that behalf, testimony under the hand and seal of the party for whom he cometh to the market to make that provision, declaring that it is for the provision of his house, and containing the quantities and kind of grain to be provided: and you shall not willingly leave any part of your corn so brought to that market unsold, if money be offered to you for the same, by any that are permitted to buy the same, after the usual price of the market there that day, as long as the market shall last.

Neither shall you from the beginning of the market, to the full end thereof, keep or cause to be kept any of your said corn out of the open sight of the market: neither shall you carry away from the market town any kind of grain that was brought thither which you have not there sold, but shall leave the same there in the market town in some place known, so long as it may be brought into the open market the next market day at the first opening of the market, there to be sold as afore was limited. And yet nevertheless, you shall bring to the market such other quantity of grain as shall be limited, and so continue at every market day the bringing into the open market, the quantity of corn that shall be limited.

Also you shall not buy any manner of such grain as the said Justices shall appoint you to sell, from this day forwards, but upon very especial and necessary cause to be allowed by them, until such time as all and every such manner grains as the said justices at this time shall appoint you to sell, be according to that appointment and order by you sold. And if you shall not sow so much this year as hath been presented that you intend to sow, or if you now have, or shall have knowledge, or shall guess hereafter at any time, either by threshing of the mow or shocks or otherwise, that you have more store of any manner of grain, then hath been presented: that then you shall forthwith upon such knowledge thereof had, make true relation thereof unto the said justices, or unto two of them, both what portion of your seed corn shall be left unsown, or what further quantity you shall perceive you have, than was at the first presented.

That so soon as you perceive you spend not after the rate of so much corn as is limited unto you for the finding of your house, you shall make true report unto the Justices or two of them, how much less you spend.

You shall buy no corn to sell it again, neither shall you by any colour directly or indirectly, appoint any your servants, or any other person to be a badger of your corn, other than to carry your corn to the market there to be sold as your own, without changing of any property.

You shall neither buy nor sell any manner of corn, but in the open market, unless the same be to some poor handicrafts men, or day labourers within the parish wherein you do dwell, that cannot conveniently come to the market towns by reason of distance of place, according to such direction as shall be given unto you in that behalf by the Justices of the Peace of that division, within which you do dwell, or two of them, & to none of these above one bushel at a time, and thereof you shall keep or cause to be kept a particular note in writing, to whom you shall so sell weekly, and at what prices, so as the same may appear to the Justices to be done without fraud or abuse.

That the Justices of the Peace within their several divisions, have special regard that Engrossers of Corn be carefully seen unto, and Inquisitions to be made for knowledge of them, and that thereupon they may be severely proceeded with and punished according to the Law and to see that none be permitted to buy any Corn to sell again, but by special License.

That they take order with the common bakers for the baking of rye, barley, peas, and beans according to the manner of the country for the use of the poor, and that they appoint special & fit persons diligently to see the people well dealt withal by the common Bakers and Brewers in all Towns and places in their Weights and Assizes, having also regard, that the Deputies of the Clerk of the Market do not abuse themselves in unlawful exactions for Weight and Measure, and effectually to enquire for and search out the default therein, and thereupon to give order for punishment of the offender severely, according to the Law: and where any notable excessive offense shall be in the Bakers, to cause the bread to be sold by them to the poorer sort under the ordinary prices, as in part of punishment of the Baker.

That no Badgers of corn, Bakers or Brewers buy any grain, or commune or bargain for the same, but in the time of open Markets, and that but by a license under the hands of the Justices of the Division where they do dwell, or three of them, and that they weekly bring their license with them to the Market where they do either buy or sell, or else not to be suffered to buy any: and that the License contain how much Grain, of what kind, and for what place they are licensed to buy and carry, that there be set down upon the License in writing, the day, place, quantity, & price at which the Corn is bought, that they take but measurably for the carriage, baking, & brewing there of, that they show their books weekly to such as the Justices of the Division wherein they dwell, shall appoint for that purpose being no Bakers or Badgers of Corn, and that those within every 14 days make report to the Justices of the Division wherein they dwell, how the people are dealt withal by the Badgers, Bakers, and Brewers, and that such as have sufficient to live on, or that are know to be of any common evil behaviour, be not permitted to be Badgers or Corn, of which sort commonly be the report is, that there are too many, and therefore the same would be remedied and foreseen: Also that no Badgers be permitted, but such as the Statute doth limit, and that no servant of any be licensed to be a Badger, except six of the Justices at the least shall in open Sessions for some necessary cause allow any such, and that none at all be allowed a badger, except he be allowed in open Sessions, and not to be, as it is in many places, abused for gain of the Clerk of the Peace, or a Justice's Clerk granted without allowance of the rest of the Justices in their open sessions, and furthermore, that none be permitted to buy or provide Corn in the Market in grosse, as a Badger or Baker, Brewer, or Purveyor and such like, upon pain of imprisonment, until two hours after the full Market be begun, that the poor may be first served.

That the said Justices, or two, or one of them at the least in every Division, shall be personally present at every Market within their several Divisions, during the whole time of the Market, to see the orders to be taken by the authority hereof to be well observed, and the poor people provided of necessary corn, and that with as much favour in the prices, as by the earnest persuasion of the Justices can be obtained. By this it is not meant to charge any Lord of Parliament, being a Justice of Peace, to attend upon any such service in any Market, otherwise then it shall be with his own good will: but in all other causes tending to the execution of these Orders, it is hoped that every person of any estate, will readily give advice and assistance.

If there shall be any Hundred, Rape or Wapentake within the said county, within the which or near thereunto no sufficient number of the said Justices of the Peace do dwell or inhabit, the said Sheriff and four Justices of the Peace of that County, shall in that case appoint some other honest Gentleman, or the high Constable, under-Constables, or such other, grave, honest, and substantial persons, not being Corn masters, dwelling within the said Hundred, Rape or Wapentake, as they shall by their discretions think convenient, to have the charge, in the execution of these orders there: whom they shall also instruct how to execute the same diligently and uprightly.

That all good means and persuasions be used by the Justices in their several divisions, & by admonitions and exhortations in Sermons in the Churches, by the Preachers and Ministers of the Word, that the poor may be served of corn at convenient & charitable prices. And to the furtherance thereof, that the richer sort be earnestly moved by Christian charity, to cause their grain to be sold under the common prices of the Market to the poorer sort: A deed of mercy, that will doubtless be rewarded of Almighty God.

That there be no buying or bargaining of any kind of Corn but in open Market, but only to poor Artificers and day Labourers, as aforesaid, and that the Justices in their several Divisions, do in convenient sort restrain common Malsters of making Barley Malt, in those countries & places where there be Oats sufficient to make malt of for the use of the people, and to restrain as well the brewing of Barley Malt, by or for Alehouses or common Tipplers in those Countries and places, as also the excess use of any kind of Malt, by all common Brewers, Malsters, and common Tipplers, according to the true meaning of this Article: and that the overabundant converting of Barley into Malt, more than may serve for necessary use, be restrained.

And where it is informed that sundry Malsters and others have already engrossed and taken into their hands great quantities of Barley, either to be converted into malt or otherwise to make their profit of it by advancing the prices thereof: It is therefore ordered that the Justices of Peace in their several Divisions, shall use all the care and diligence they may, to find out such engrossers, and to examine them exactly how much of such kind of Corn they have already in their hands, or have compounded for, and at what price, and where it is. And thereupon the said Justices of the Peace to take order that so much thereof in Barley as shall be thought fit in the direction of the same Justices, be brought to such of the next Markets thereunto, as the same Justices shall assign, there to be sold to the poor people of the Town and Country adjoining, by the sack or coomb, or lesser quantity, and by no greater quantity to any one person at such reasonable price, and with such reasonable gain as the same Justices shall think fit. And such as shall be found obstinate to obey this order, to be bound with good sureties to answer the matter before the Lords of his Majesty's Privy Council at some day to be prefixed by the same Justices. And the great number of Malsters to be reduced to fewer persons, & such as have other trades to live by, not to be permitted to use malting.

That the Justices use all other good means possible that are not mentioned in these orders, that the Markets may be well served, and the poor relieved in their provisions during this time of Dearth. And that no expense of any Grain meet for bread to feed men, be wasted upon feeding of dogs or other beasts, neither that any be spent in making stuff called Starch.

That the Justices be straightly commanded to see by all good means, that the able people be set on work in houses of Correction provided and furnished, and their idle vagabonds to be punished.

That the Justices do their best to have convenient stocks of money or wares, to be provided in every Division, or other places according to the Statute, for setting the poor on work, and the Justices to use all other good & politique means within their several Divisions, to continue and maintain the poor people in work within the Parish, or at the furthest within the Hundred, or Division, and namely in clothing Countries to charge the Clothiers, that have in former times gained by that trade, not now in this time of dearth to leave off his trade, whereby the poor may be set on work.

That the maimed and hurt Soldier, and all other impotent persons be carefully seen unto to be relieved within their several Parishes, Hundreds or Divisions, according to the Law therein provided: and that where the provisions formerly made, and assessed upon the householders in every Parish be not sufficient, it may be now for this time of dearth charitably increased. And where any parish is not able to give sufficient relief to such their poor, that parish to have the supply of such other parishes near adjoining, as have fewer poor, and are better able to give relief. And no vagabond or sturdy beggar, or any that may otherwise get their living by their labours, be suffered to wander abroad under colour of begging in any town, field or highway, & that the Justices do presently give order that there be able persons appointed, & sufficiently weaponed, to assist the Constables of every Town to attach such vagabonds, both in their town, fields and highways to commit them to prison without bail of any such, but as two of the Justices of the Peace within that Division shall order. And if any Township shall not observe this order, for the attaching and punishing of the said vagabonds, then the Justices shall set due punishment by fine upon the whole Township, or upon such parties in the Town, as shall be found in fault.

Where in some parts of the realm, divers Millers, who ought only to serve for grinding of corn that shall be brought to their mills, have begun lately a very corrupt trade to be common buyers of Corn, both in markets, and out of markets, and the same do grind into meal, and do use as Badgers, or otherwise to sell the same at markets and in other places, seeking thereby an inordinate gain, besides the mis-using of other men's corn brought thither to be ground, by delay of grinding, or that worse is, by changing & altering of their good corn to the worse: It is thought very necessary, that the Justices of the Peace who are not owners by any title of any Mills, nor masters or landlords to any millers, shall first inhibit all millers upon pain both of imprisonment & fine, to use any such trade of buying of any grain to be sold either in corn or Meal, but to charge them, to continue the orderly use of grinding of all manner of Corn that shall be brought to them, in reasonable good sort, & upon reasonable Toll. And for better performance hereof some of the Justices not affectionated to the Millers, shall sometime personally themselves resort to the Mills to oversee the doings of the said Millers, and compel them to do their duties. And where none of the Justices can, as need shall be, weekly look thereunto personally, they shall appoint certain honest persons weekly to attend thereto, and to inform themselves of the poorer sort, how they are used in this time of dearth, for their grinding and their Toll, and present the defaults to the Justices, to be speedily reformed with all due severity.

Item, where there are within the circuit of any Shire, or thereto adjoining, any Cities that are incorporated as Towns within themselves, or any other

Towns incorporate, that have by good authority Justices of Peace of their own inhabitants, for that commonly such Cities and Towns have their greatest number of householders that are no owners of grain, but have common Bakers, and Brewers, that must of necessity buy and provide their Corn or Meal at the Markets near thereto, to serve all other the inhabitants & residents within the said Cities and Towns: for the provision of all such Cities and Towns, it shall be necessary that the Justices of the Peace of the Shires next to the same Cities and Towns, shall have a meeting and conference with the head Officers of the said Cities & Towns, how and in what good manner the Bakers and Brewers, and other householders that shall also have need to provide Corn or Meal for the necessary use of the private households may be provided at the Markets near to the same. And after due conference had hereof, there shall be by the Justices of Peace, and the foresaid head Officers some good orders set down, such as both may serve for the needful use of the same Towns and Cities, & also may not by abuse give cause of raising of prices in the markets & Countries adjoining. And where there shall be adjoining to the same Cities & Towns, or not far distant, divers Shires (as in many places such is the situation of them) there some of the Justices of every Shire so adjoining, or not far distant, shall use such conference and take such order with the said Officers, as afore is mentioned. And in such cases the Justices of every such Shire shall be informed mutually from the one Shire unto the other, of the needful provisions to be made from time to time for the said Cities and Towns, so as every Shire may proportionally yield reasonable succour and relief out of their Markets to the Purveyors, or to the Bakers and Brewers, as shall be requisite without burthening of the one, more than the other may reasonably bear. And if need shall require, the aforesaid principal Officers shall not refuse to acquaint the Justices, from whence the provision shall be bought and provided, how such provision so had & bought in Markets are spent, that by colour of such provisions no abuse be committed to increase the prices, and so to leave the poor unable to be relieved.

If there be any special part within any Shire, that hath as a liberty by Special Commissions any Justices of the Peace within the same, the Sheriff of the Shire shall send unto the Principal owner or Officer of such Liberty, notice of these orders, & shall charge them that the Justices of the Peace within such Liberty do their duties for execution of all these orders, as far forth as shall be requisite, and therein also to use by conference the advice of some other Justices next adjoining.

That no transportation of Corn or Victual be, but from port to port within this Realm, and that but in cases needful, as for the provisions of London, shipping or such like. And that be done by the view and overseeing of his Majesty's officers of the Custom house of the port, where the same shall be laden, or of the most part of them, of the chief Magistrates of the Town in which that Port is, also of some of the Commissioners of the county in which that port is, and for that purpose assigned. And that in such case good bonds with sufficient sureties be taken to his Majesty's use for the delivery thereof at the port to which the same shall be assigned. And for bringing back in convenient time not only a true Certificate of the unlading thereof at the same port so assigned from his Majesty's officers of the Custom house of that port, to the Customer of the port where the same was laden: But also one other certificate from the chief Magistrate of the Town of that port where the same shall be assigned to be unladen: And from some of the Commissioners of the County in which that Town is, for the purpose assigned unto the Commissioners and chief Magistrate of that port where the same was laden, of the due and just unlading thereof at the port assigned. And transcripts of those Certificate to be made and certified unto the Exchequer in the beginning of every Term.

And if the Commissioners for that purpose assigned, shall not do their best endeavours to make stay of the transporting of Corn, as by authority of their Commission they ought to do, then any other Justice by authority of these Orders shall make stay of all such transportation, and in his doing, shall be allowed and maintained. And this is thought meet to be in this sort directed, for that it may be doubted that amongst so many as are appointed in the foresaid Commission against transportation, some may be mistaken, being themselves either transporters, or negligent in the execution of the charge committed to them.

That the Justices of the Peace do once every month certify their doings and proceedings by force of these Instructions unto the Sheriff of the said County, in which certificate they shall also make certificate of such Justices as shall be absent from any of these securities, and the true cause of their absence, and shall also certify the usual prices of all kinds of Grain in their Markets for that month past: Of all which the same Sheriff shall certify to the Privy Council without any delay, so as he do certify once in every forty days at the furthest, and so as also the default in any Justice that shall be absent without necessary cause, may be duly considered, and reformed by authority of his Majesty's Council, as reason shall require: whereby such persons as are placed as Justices, may not continue in those rooms wherein they shall be found not disposed to attend such necessary and godly services as this is, but that others of better disposition may supply those rooms, if there shall be need of any such number.

Special enquiry be made of those that are great hoarders up of corn, and bring little quantity to the Market, to the end from such person's provision may be made for his Majesty's shipping, and other public services, as need shall require.

And if any shall offend against the true meaning of these Instructions, or of any part thereof, or shall use any sinister means to the defrauding thereof, that such be severely punished according to the Laws: and for such obstinate persons as shall not conform themselves, the Justices shall at their discretion bind them to appear before the King's Majesty's Privy Council by a day certain, there to be further dealt with by severe punishment, for the better example of all others.

Item, the Justices shall take order that the multitude of Badgers & Bakers both of Butter and Cheese, as also of Corn to sell again, may in every County upon conference among the Justices be reduced to a competent number, and those of the fittest persons for that purpose, and the residue to be removed.

That such of these Badgers and Bakers as shall remain, be only permitted to make provision to furnish the Markets of such Cities and other great Towns and places which otherwise are not able to be sufficiently provided for, of those provision in the Countries near adjoining, for that they are only needful for those places.

That the Farmer or Malster be not permitted to sell to any such Badgers or Buyer, nor to any such Badgers or Buyer, nor to any Baker or Brewer out of a Market, nor that any Badgers or Buyers to sell again, be permitted to buy any Corn, Butter or Cheese, but in the Market: Neither any Baker, Brewer, Badger or such Buyer as aforesaid to sell again; be permitted to buy in any Market but two hours at the least after the full of the Market, whereby others may be served of their particular provisions: And then the Badger, Baker, & Buyer to sell again, to take away the intplusage of the Market only.

To foresee that no covenous practices be used between the farmer or Malster, and the Badger, Broker, Brewer, or Buyer to sell again, whereby the Farmer or other should detain his Corn or Malt to the end of the Market to the hindrance of the Market: But if any such be found, then such offender to be duly punished.

Higglers and Purveyors for the City of London or any other city, not to be permitted to buy Corn or other victual but in open Market, and that two hours after the full market, whereby the poorer sort may be served of that which they shall need at competent prices: Nevertheless, for the better furnishing of your said Cities with necessary provisions and in convenient manner, it is ordered that further provisions shall be from time to time made for them in such sort as the Lords of his Majesty's Council shall further direct in that behalf.

It is also ordered, that the feeding of sheep with peas or beans which is used in some countries for food be specially forbidden, because in time of dearth the same may serve the poorer sort to make bread of.

That there be monthly a view taken what Corn any farmer or other person using to sell Corn, hath both threshed, and by estimation in the stoage, and to be enjoined to sell none but in open Market, except to poor artificers and day labourers their neighbours, and to yield a due account to the Justices, of the expense of his Corn, and how much he doth sell weekly in any Market.

That inquisition be made in what places Malt is commonly made to be sold by such as are called Malsters, and who they be. And to take order, that by buying and engrossing of barley to make malt, they do not thereby store by greater quantity of malt than they usually bring into the Markets, thereby towards the end of the year to increase the price thereof excessively. Of which abuse the Justices are to take care to reform the same, and to take order also that they shall buy their Barley in open Market, and not at the farmer's houses, thereby to forestall the Markets, and to enhance the prices.

To take strait order with the common Brewers, that they serve no Beer or Ale to any Alehousekeeper, Victualler, or Tippler, but at such rate and price as by the Justices of the Peace shall set down and appointed by authority of the

Statute of 23 H.8 cap.4. And yet the same to be well sodden and well brewed of wholesome grain as it ought to be, upon pain of [blank] to be imposed by the Justices.

That Alehousekeepers suffer none to eat and tipple, or victual in their houses, but such as are wayfaring men, that shall take the same to refresh themselves in their passage or journey, or such as shall be appointed to lodge or take diet in their houses, but to deliver out of their houses that quantity of drink which their neighbours of the poorer sort shall have need of, to be drunk in the houses of those who fetch or send for the same and not elsewhere.

To permit no tippling at all on the Sabbath day, or holy day in time of Divine service.

That no victualler, Tippler or Alehousekeeper, shall permit and suffer any person or persons to lodge in his house above a day and a night, but such as he will answer for, as the Statutes in that behalf made do require.

To give straight order and charge to every constable, or other inferior Officer to whom it may appertain, that every of them shall once in every fifteen days search and enquire of the defaults and disorders aforesaid, and shall inform the Justices of the Peace of the same defaults and disorders if any be, that the offenders therein may thereupon be proceeded on and punished according to the Law. And if it shall seem to the Justice, that the Petty Constable be either a victualer, or one that shall favour the victualers in their faults, then some other meet person to be appointed to make the said Inquisition and Certificate.

No Tippler to buy any goods of any Wayfaring man, or other, that shall bring the same to their houses to sell, but of such as shall be well known unto them to be of honest conversation, and whom they shall be able always to produce, or have to be forthcoming.

GLOSSARY

badger	a middleman between the producer and consumer
brewster	a brewer
brogger	an agent
coomb	a dry measure of four bushels
engrosser	one who buys all supplies of a commodity wholesale in order to retail it a monopoly price
forestaller	one who intercepts goods before they reach public markets with a view to enhance the price
higgler	an itinerant dealer
jowter(or jouster)	a hawker of fish
kiddier	one who buys provisions from the producers and takes them to market to be sold
mow	a stack of hay, corn, beans, peas, etc; a heap of grain or hay in a barn
mowhay	a loft of chamber for storing grain in Cornwall and Devon
pilchard	a mature sardine
pillas	a type of oats grown especially in Cornwall and Devon
regrater	one who buys up supplies of a commodity for re-sale in the same or near-by market
stoage	a place where goods are stored
tippler	a retailer of ale and other intoxicating beverages
tippling house	a house where intoxicating liquor is sold and consumed
victuals	provisions
wotts	obscure form of oats

INDEX OF PLACE-NAMES
The numbers refer to documents and not to page numbers

INDEX OF PERSONAL-NAMES

The numbers refer to documents and not to page numbers

SUBSCRIBERS

John H. Andrew
Tom Arkell
Dr J R Barber
D Barthold
Lt. Cdr. John W. Beck R.N.
A.J. Bissett
A. Blackman
M.W. Blake
Dr David P. Blight
John Blowey
Kelvin Boot
C.J. Borlase
Dr Mark Brayshay
Mr C.W. Brewer
Frank L. Brewer
S.A. Butcher
Callington Local Hist.Group
Mrs Janet Cambridge
Mrs Veronica M. Chesher
Paul D. Cockerham
Mrs Jacqueline Collins
Cookworthy Museum
F.B.J. Coombes
Mr G.V. Coon
Cornwall County Libraries
David J. Corney
Courtney Library
Mrs I. Cox
T.O. Darke
B.W. Deacon
James Derriman

Devon & Exeter Institution
H.L. Douch
J.C. Edwards
Mrs S.R. Ford
Dr H.S.A. Fox
Miss M. Garland
H.W. Gill
Peter Gilson
Bill Glanville
Mrs G.G. Green
Mrs P.M. Griffith
Dr F.L. Harris
Mrs Jean Haigh
F.G. Hamlyn
Keith Hamylton-Jones
Mrs P.L. Hanwell
Miss C.E. Harry
Mr S.J. Hawke
Mr S. Hebdige

Mr & Mrs G.S. Henwood
Daphné Hicks
R.B.N. Hicks
Norman Hicks
Mrs Marie High
Mr J.C. Hockin
Mr J. Hodge
N.E. Hoskin
Mrs R. Howells
J.C. & J.C.M. Ivey
Robert Jago
L.R. James
W.J. James
Miss J.M.E. Jellie
Mr A.W. Jenkyn
Mr N. Johnson
Dr Malcolm D. Jones
Revd Barry Kinsmen
John F. Lavelle
J.G.W. Lewarne
Trevor Lloyd
Malcolm McCarthy
Mrs B Mann
Mr E.A. Martin
M.J. Martyn
D.H. Michell
Mr & Mrs L.W. Michell
Mrs Joy Miller
Mrs J. Moore
Mr D.F. Mitchell
Jean Nankervis
Newquay Old Cornwall Society
Mrs A.J. Nicholls
Mr & Mrs E. Nicholls
N.Devon Libr. & Record Office
Dr M. Overton
Mrs June Palmer
Mr P. Parsons
Dr Philip Payton
B.R. Peeke
Mrs P. Penhallurick
F.M. Penwarden
Mary Peter
Revd W.M.M. Picken
Steven Pugsley
Tom Rankin
Mr Roff Rayner
Felicity Richards
Mrs J.F. Riley
Mr W.H. Roberts

P. Rose
Mrs R.M. Royle
Mrs R.J. Roseveare
Dr M. Rundle
D.A. Sandy
Mr Alan Saville
J. Scantlebury
Dr Brian Selwood
Dr P.A. Slack
J.L. Smedley
Mrs Marion Smith
Revd M.G. Smith
Colin J. Squires
R.G.F. Stanes
Mark Stoyle
Mrs M.M. Spear
Mrs Moira Tangye
Shirley Todman
Mr J.W.S. Thomas
Paul Thomas
Hilary Thompson
P.F. Thorning
Mr P.J. Towey
R.R. Trebilcock
David Treffry
Michael Trinick
Miss B.J. Tripp
L.H. Truran
John Tyacke
Mr J.M. Uren
University of Leicester Library
Mr D. Vanstone
Mrs E. Vogwill
Martin Wagrel
Mrs F.S. Walker
L.B. Ward
Mr R.O. Warmington
Revd James West
Dr E.A.O. Whiteman
Mr A.J. Williams
Mrs M. Williams
Professor Joyce Youings